Yeshua the Cosmic Mystic

Beyond Religion to Universal Truth

By

Theodore J. Nottingham

A special expression of gratitude for the gracious and generous assistance of Kathleen Marie Brown for her expertise in editing the transcribed portions of this book and bringing polish and ease of reading to you who pick up this book.

ISBN 978-0983769736

Cover Art:
Pillars of Creation
Hubble Telescope
Icon from the Hagia Sophia

Printed in the United States of America.

Table of Contents

PART III   Deep Waters

Foreword

The religion that arose in the wake of the appearance of Yeshua the Nazarene and his radical wisdom teachings has been morphing for 2000 years. The institutions and hierarchies which were created, often according to secular models, especially in the West, transformed the instructions for experience of the Holy into creeds and dogmas that were no longer about intimate personal encounter and transformation. That disconnection with the Source -- the original teachings -- fragmented the Truth as shared by the Anointed One into a religion that stood over against other religions and other belief systems.

Rather than finding the Oneness of the heart of humanity's deepest intuitions and highest insights of mind and heart, the "Christian" religion generated wars and turned into a wall that divided the mind and heart, and the inner and outer life. The surface version of this crystallized container of the original teachings became an oppressive force, often crushing and burying alive the human spirit. According to whatever powers were in charge across the centuries, individuals were tortured, excommunicated, burned and killed in countless ways because they did not fit the false and artificial mold that claimed to contain the spiritual truth made known by the one called Yeshua (Hebrew, meaning "God is salvation").

Until recently, the West knew nothing of the Eastern Church whose roots were more ancient and held closer to the beginnings, to the Source, and had entirely different views on the purpose and teachings of the Christ. Later, the Reformation fragmented the teachings into hundreds of different versions. For centuries, people in the West did not even know what was contained in Holy Scripture, but received from the Church, in a foreign language, the version the Hierarchy chose to dispense to them.

The Reformation was born out of the awareness of the indwelling of the Holy Spirit in each person. But instead of liberating the spiritual wisdom and truth found at the heart of the teachings, it shattered into a thousand theologies the original spark that came out of that small group from Galilee. It wasn't until the end of the nineteenth century that different gospels were uncovered, bringing to light other understandings of the original wisdom made known by the Anointed One. Near the middle of the twentieth century, a treasure trove of ancient texts, deeply beloved by early Christian communities, revealed a very different kind of transformational wisdom. Certainly, much fantasy and mythology were mixed in, but in essence it was clear that during the infancy of Christianity, for the "People of the Way," there were very different experiences and perspectives on what the teachings were meant to convey. This is especially true for the Gospel of Thomas which is generally regarded as an earlier record of the teachings and source material for the familiar four Gospels of the New Testament. In these sayings, we find an extraordinary mystical wisdom and revelation that touches on the eternal and universal dimensions of the mission of the Christ.

In typical rational fashion, the academics and rigid thinkers have categorized these discoveries into gnostic and orthodox groupings, rejecting the one for the other. In fact, many modern academics do not even believe in the orthodox creeds, yet they still reject the gnostic teachings. So two thousand years later, in this global community of ours, this religion is in danger of total disintegration and collapsing into a distorted ruin of what was once vibrant Truth and a revelation of a life-giving wisdom meant to be conveyed across the centuries to every human being.

It is rather straightforward: If indeed Yeshua bar Joseph brought into our world a new consciousness of the nature of reality, the nature of the Uncreated One and of our own identity, then such Truth transcends all cultures, traditions and times. The fact is that such revelation is either beyond time, and holistic in all its implications, or it is not Truth at all.

This book is meant to assist the reader in rediscovering, beyond tired vocabulary and oppressive experiences, the spiritual teachings that contain true and transformative content. Such a journey is possible because, ultimately, the Teacher -- the Cosmic Christ -- is the incarnation of our ultimate purpose and identity, and can be found at the very roots of our being, in the most intimate center of our spirit.

Our very hunger for such life-changing Truth is already guidance from the Spirit realm from which we originate, and our resonance to what seems right to us can be trusted if there is purity in our motive. Even in calling for this new holistic understanding of the original teachings, which from the very beginning were misunderstood and turned into weapons against each other, this book is not meant to water down the significance and uniqueness of the Yeshua event.

Clearly one can recognize similar wisdom in the great teachers of humanity all across the world and learn from them. But in that exceptional, self-sacrificial and unconditional love demonstrated by the Man from Nazareth, we find the ultimate focus, surrender, and unity with the Presence of the Holy. Because of that personal and intimate reconnection that links each person to the heart of spiritual Reality, every human being is given great value, and is revealed as a potential incarnation of the Sacred, and a carrier of blessing to humanity.

There is no more potent transformational wisdom than the teachings of Yeshua unadulterated by human misunderstandings, literalism, rationalization and other perversions. Seekers of Truth who journey with integrity, free from prejudices, will recognize in the mystics of various traditions, traces uniting them in common experiences. This book is not suggesting that the reader disregard the obscene sacrilegious and blasphemous misrepresentations of Christianity that have emerged down through time and are found in churches everywhere to this very day. Indeed, one section of this work is devoted to confirming this fact in very personal and tragic ways. But the outer form, and the abuses and ignorance of human beings, are irrelevant to anyone who is truly seeking the experiential Presence of the Holy here and now as made known and accessible by the Anointed One.

Introduction

The Neglected Heart of Religion

"Better to be cast out of the Church than to deny God."
Anne Hutchinson before her judges in 1638

Strangely enough, the Christian faith has long held a schizophrenic relationship with the mystical dimension of its own teachings. The very nature of this religion, which claims that God became a human being so that human beings could become godlike (as stated by one of the early teachers) is, above all, a teaching on mysticism -- linking the material and spiritual worlds in an intimate, interconnected bond.

Across every century, Christianity has given birth to some of the world's greatest mystics, people who have experienced a dimension of reality that is universal and true for all people, revealing some of the mysteries of why we exist and who we are beyond our culturally acquired identities. And yet, the Church has often condemned the very best representatives of its tradition. Why? The answer is painfully simple. The mystics were a threat to the authority and structure of the institution. When it is suggested that any person can have direct access to the dimension of the Holy, then what becomes of the priests and clergy who serve as professional intercessors? A lot of people would be out of work...and maybe should be if they are not true spiritual teachers.

There is also another reason, exemplified in the case of the great Meister Eckhart, one of the giants of the Christian mystical tradition. One of his students, John Tauler who was a mystic in his own right, stated that "he spoke to you from the point of view of eternity and you understood him from the point of view of time."

The sad fact is that the enlightened perceptions of these profound individuals could not be grasped by leaders of the Church who dealt in platitudes and superficial dogma. The Church excommunicated this German Master (even though he claimed to be its loyal son to the end of his days) because his experience of God soared so high that it transcended the need for priests and sacraments. Everything he wrote concerning the encounter with the Divine was based on immediate, personal experience, and that is why he is as vital a guide at the end of the twentieth century as he was at the beginning of the fourteenth.

The times in which he spoke were very much like our own. A great spiritual upheaval was taking place. There was a movement called "Liberty of Spirit," ancestor to our New Age approach to awakening; there was also a new "awakening" brought by the discovery of Arabic, Hebrew and Greek thought which was causing people to found their beliefs on reason as well as on the heart; at the same time, universities were packed with pedantic, hair-splitting academics, utterly insulated from the life-giving depths of the Faith; the Church itself had lost prestige as the Pope's authority was called into question, and the selling of indulgences made grotesquely clear the financial lusts of the institution.

Finally, a great many lay movements were arising in reaction to the sterile teachings of Rome. Men and women who were seeking the living waters of spiritual consciousness came together to create loosely connected groups such as *The Friends of God* and magnificent works like *The Imitation of Christ*, *Theologia Germanica*, and Mechtild of Magdeburg's *The Light of the Godhead*. The visionaries born from the religious turmoil of the fourteenth century, Jacob Boheme, Hildegard of Bingen, John Ruysbroeck, and Julian of Norwich, were all influenced by the mighty spiritual light of Meister Eckhart, whose wisdom remains timeless and still enlightens contemporary seekers.

He left us with these words, which come close to a Zen koan, suggesting that in resolving the paradoxes, we find the answers: *"You ought to sink down out of all your your-ness, and flow into his his-ness, and your 'yours' and his 'his' ought to become one 'mine,' so completely that you with him perceive forever his uncreated is-ness, and his nothingness, for which there is no name."*

One of the highly respected personalities in the religious world of our time, the monk Bede Griffith, made this radical and prophetic statement late in his life: *"If Christianity cannot recover its mystical tradition and teach it, it should just fold up and go out of business."*

There is no question that should Christianity not recover the essence of its purpose -- which is the awakening of the spiritual depths of human beings in a way that utterly transforms their understanding of themselves and their relationship with life -- then it will have completely failed in its mission and will have nothing to offer a world that desperately needs a unifying vision and a sense of common ground among people and cultures. It is the mystic, first and foremost, who reveals the spiritual home that we all share and the wondrous purpose of our presence in the universe.

PART I

WISDOM TEACHINGS

1

Then God Said...
Redefining the Great Misunderstanding

Then God said, 'Let us make humankind in our image, according to our likeness; and let them have dominion over the fish of the sea, and over the birds of the air, and over the cattle, and over all the wild animals of the earth, and over every creeping thing that creeps upon the earth.' (Genesis 1:26)

From the beginning, these words of Genesis have established in the human mind a sense of ownership, of superiority and authority over everything else in creation. This presumed relationship to the world around us has been a cornerstone of domination, exploitation, abuses of every kind, and violence and destruction on an unimaginable scale. However one generation chose to interpret those revered words *"let them have dominion,"* the results have always been the same -- I can do whatever I want with this because I am divinely appointed to dominate it. From this viewpoint has come a litany of horrors from slavery to deforestation and the current human-induced ecological crises.

Other key Old Testament passages have molded our relationship to nature in ways that we are often unconscious of and which we take for granted:

The fear and dread of you shall rest on every animal of the earth, and on every bird of the air, on everything that creeps on the ground, and on all the fish of the sea; into your hand they are delivered. Every moving thing that lives shall be food for you; and just as I gave you the green plants, I give you everything. (Genesis 9:2,3)

Is it not obvious how imperialism, colonialism, ecological genocide and even ethnic cleansing have been justified and enabled by such deeply embedded assumptions?

It is time to ask ourselves as a species if we have perhaps misinterpreted these ancient words and victimized nature and all living things far too long. This idea of "dominion" is a profoundly anti-spiritual concept. The universal spiritual teachings of humanity unite in their common wisdom at the level of mystical experience and they have always given us a different picture of our relationship to the world. Consider Francis of Assisi and his words on "brother sun, sister moon." All those who have been considered saints or "holy" have been lovers of nature. Their insights are crucial to a right relationship with our environment and even to our basic understanding of reality.

In this day and age, these spiritual perceptions of our interconnectedness with the world around us are being confirmed by the latest scientific explorations. Ideas like string theory, supersymmetry, and emergence, all suggest a fundamental symbiotic relationship among all living things. Cutting-edge quantum physicists are pointing to an organizing principle, or what some are calling a "conscious substructure," upholding and sustaining the fabric of our universe. This phenomenon, at the heart of all things and yet greater than all that is created, is obviously that which we simply call "God." If such is the case, then clearly this uncreated aspect of reality is not suggesting to humanity that we trash the universe any way we wish. For in doing so, we are trashing the immanent Sacred as well.

The Hebrew word translated as "dominion" is *radah*. It is only used a dozen times in the Old Testament and has a special meaning. In the book of Ezekiel, we find it used in a negative way which is rejected by God: *You have not strengthened the weak, you have not healed the sick, you have not bound up the injured, you have not brought back the strayed, you have not sought the lost, but with force and harshness you have ruled [radah] them. (Ezekiel 34:4)* This is a clear denunciation of dominion wrongly expressed.

The *radah* that humanity is called to have over creation is to *strengthen and heal and bind*. In other words, we are to deal with nature and all living beings as their Creator would deal with them. We are to incarnate the cosmic goodness that generated all that is for the purpose of caretaking. We are the caretakers of nature, not its oppressors. This is a very far cry from "dominion" as it has been understood for thousands of years.

2

The Heart of the Teaching

One of the scribes came near and heard them disputing with one another, and seeing that He answered them well, he asked him, "Which commandment is the first of all?" Jesus answered, "The first is, 'Hear, O Israel: the Lord our God, the Lord is one; you shall love the Lord your God with all your heart, and with all your soul, and with all your mind, and with all your strength.' The second is this, 'You shall love your neighbor as yourself.' There is no other commandment greater than these."

Then the scribe said to Him, "You are right, Teacher; you have truly said that 'he is one, and besides him there is no other;' and 'to love him with all the heart, and with all the understanding, and with all the strength,' and 'to love one's neighbor as oneself,' — this is much more important than all whole burnt offerings and sacrifices." When Jesus saw that he had answered wisely, He said to him, "You are not far from the kingdom of God." And after that no one dared to ask Him any question. (Mark 12: 28-34)

This small section of scripture is truly powerful. Let's make no mistake about it, it's deeply important. This is the heart of the teaching, the heart of the message, not only of Christ, but even of the Old Testament. If we get this one right, we have a compass for understanding all other aspects of the teachings.

To put it in context, Jesus has been in Jerusalem for a week and the Pharisees, Sadducees, and elders -- the religious people -- are out to trip him up, to entrap him. Here we have a great paradox: Jesus versus religion. How is that for a strange idea? In Matthew 22, where the story is also told, we find these words: *"The Pharisees, having seen that Jesus silenced the Sadducees, assembled together..."* Don't you know that we human beings like to get together in little groups to connive and manipulate, to backstab, to plot and all those dark things that are so ungodly?

In Matthew we find that the Pharisees -- the teachers of the law, the scholars, the ones who have it right -- are going to find a way to get him. But here in Mark we have a slightly different perspective. Did you see how the scribe who is a scholar of the Law (the Torah), seeing that He answered rightly, goes to Him? This is a scholar who knows the Law and realizes that this man standing before him just might have an answer for the hunger in his soul. He has made the discovery that knowing the sacred Laws of his religion and Moses' teachings about God, were not enough.

Sometimes knowledge is not enough. The Chosen People, those who gave monotheism to the world, who left child sacrifice behind and led humanity on a journey of enlightened understanding, had developed through their priests some 613 laws. Of these, 365 were prohibitions, "Thou shall not," and 248 were "Thou shall...do this." The scholars knew them all and assumed that Jesus might get 612 wrong if they asked him the question. So there was a good chance they could get him on a technicality because their religion had been reduced to proper ritual, proper theology, proper doctrine and proper memorization, and the spirit was gone.

As the Apostle Paul said: *"The Letter kills but the Spirit gives life."* The prophets knew this from ancient times. We find Hosea saying, *"I prefer mercy not sacrifice,"* and by sacrifice he meant the proper way to conduct worship in those times according to cultic law. Isaiah cries out: *"These people honor me with their lips, but their hearts are far from me."* He is not talking about Israelites long ago who became confused and lost. He is talking about you and me right now, today. Is your heart far from God while you worship God? Is there hate? Is there division? Is there unrighteous behavior that is displeasing to God right now? Are you a Pharisee who wants to make sure that we get it right or else?

When Jesus says, "Hear, O Israel," understand that he is talking to those of us in this day and age who yearn for the experience of the Presence of God, who, in spite of our culture and our peers, believe in the deeper reality of the Sacred at the heart of existence. *"Hear, you who love God,"* he says, followed by: *"The Lord our God is one..."* In Hebrew, the word for "one" is *"Echad,"* and it not only means "one," it also means *reliable*. The Living, Uncreated One is reliable, enabling each of us to respond in love, gratitude and remembrance with "all your heart and mind and soul and strength."

In Hebrew, the heart is understood as the center of our being. The soul is the willpower to make choices. Jesus leaps over all the obligations and requirements of religion, and goes directly to the key issue. Remember, he is the one who said, *"It doesn't matter what goes into your mouth but what comes out of it."* He breaks all the kosher and dietary laws, the very identity of what it means to be Hebrew and part of the Chosen People. This is blasphemy for the religious, but Jesus came to upset the applecart! Louis Evely, the Belgian priest, wrote that Jesus did not come to create a new religion. Rather, he came to give us *direct access to God,* past all the mumbo-jumbo and the human-made creeds that have made religion such a disaster in human history.

We are told: "The Lord our God is One." What is the implication of God's oneness? This is nothing less than quantum physics. It means that if God is one, then we are one. Reality is all interconnected. We are all interconnected at the subatomic levels. We are one, and when we proclaim God's oneness, we proclaim our unity in spite of all that is set up to separate us.

"You shall love Him with all your heart and mind and soul and strength." Some folks love God emotionally and that's a wonderful thing. They get goose bumps at beautiful music or they go to some big mega-church with all kinds of instruments and feel great when they leave. But what happens when the emotional high is over and they calm down? You know what happens? They're just tired then. To love God only according to our emotional states is an up and down, inconstant thing. It has to be part of a bigger whole: "with all your..." *All* in Greek is *"holos,"* meaning holistically, with all the different aspects of ourselves. There are people who love God intellectually. They have read every book they can get their hands on. They are encyclopedias of religious information, but like that scribe in the teaching, they *do not know* God. They do not have relationship with living Spirit.

It can be compared to a person who reads all about flying, but has never flown a plane. Do you want to get on that plane? Each of us is guilty in our own way because each of us has our particular approach to dealing with life intellectually, emotionally, or physically. Yet all of who we are needs to be integrated into worship or consciousness of God. This is the following of Christ's Way.

On the American frontier, something happened called *bibliolatry*, where the book became a magic book and the worship was of the book, not of the Spirit revealed through the book.

Jesus calls us to have discernment. The Old Testament, with the God of the Hebrews who wanted to kill the children of the Canaanites, is an earlier understanding of the nature of God revealed by Jesus. We went from child sacrifice to worshipping at the high places with the sacrificing of animals, and finally to ultimate awakening to the reality of God through Christ.

We must look at these teachings through the eyes of Christ, and when we don't, when we take it all as the same kind of teaching, we fail to understand what he is telling us -- that none of those 613 sacred laws matter if we don't love the

Lord our God with all our heart, mind, and soul in such a way that we are transformed. How easy, how human it is to reduce religion to performing certain acts and rituals properly so that we can feel good about ourselves.

In ancient times the Hebrews, with all their sacred laws, assumed that *if we get this many right and this many wrong, we can balance it all out and be accessible to Yahweh in the long run.* This was a form of bargaining with God, but the new teaching from Yeshua calls for all or nothing. Then he tells us about that second teaching, "Love your neighbor as yourself." Let's not take that so lightly, or skip over it so quickly. This comes out of Leviticus 19:18: *"Do not seek revenge or bear a grudge against one of your people but love your neighbor as yourself. I am the Lord."* Modern day Hebrew teachers will tell you that the word "neighbor" in Leviticus is *"rei'acha"* which means *close companion,* sometimes translated as "spouse." They claim that it does not mean everyone universally, and so they translate it *"Love your (fellow Jew) neighbor. Love your family. Love your tribe."*

This is where a new enlightenment is made known through the Christ, one that is indeed universal rather than tribal or familial. This is why the Christ had to come. This is why the prophets were pushing further and further towards that time of true enlightenment and awakening to God's call on our lives. The Hebrews tell us that *"shachen"* is the word for neighbor and it is not listed there in the origins of this teaching. So in the Old Testament, "Love your neighbor" was "Love your fellow villager," whereas we know through the parable of the good Samaritan and all the teachings of Christ that when he says "Love your neighbor," he means every human being.

But more than that, this spiritual teaching is not, as some might suppose, *"Well, I love myself so I will love you a little too."* No, Jesus is saying: "Love your neighbor as though he or she *were yourself.* See that which is divine in the other person as the divine is within you. See that oneness of God in that other person and in you." That is the Christ consciousness awakened in humanity. That is breaking through the boundaries of "us against them," of primitive thinking, of separation. That is radical living. That is seeing the divine everywhere.

The Hebrews, in their spiritual evolution, spoke of "fragments of the divine" broken like a mirror throughout Creation, and our work is to recognize these fragments and pull them back together into their original unity. Yet, even with that deep wisdom, the neighbor was the fellow Jew, not the Gentile. It took this extraordinary, totally transforming Way of Christ that could not be held in a cultural box, nor in a religion, to break through to a new kind of understanding. He not only fulfills the Laws (the Torah, more accurately translated as "Instructions"), but he transforms them so that what matters is unconditional love coming through us, that we might be benediction to the world, children of God who are conscious of our origin, our purpose, and our destiny. That is the religion (meaning "re-linking") that Jesus brought, reconnecting us to Spirit.

Beyond all the structures, dogmas, rules and theologies is the one thing that matters -- the compass that Jesus gives us today. As it is written in the Scriptures, they dared not ask him anymore questions after that. Those waters were too deep.

3

The Mystic Roots of Christianity

The word "church" is a translation combining several Greek words and a multitude of images and metaphors. It comes directly from a word meaning "those who belong to God." The New Testament writers used many descriptions to express the meaning of church: slaves of Christ, the people of God, the family of God, the bride of Christ, or the body of Christ. In the Book of Acts, the term "brothers" is used thirty times to describe the fellowship we call church.

Church is therefore a gathering of individuals who, called together by a stirring in their hearts, seek to awaken to the divine presence. The real building of the church is, in the words of Thomas Merton, "a union of hearts in love, sacrifice, self-transcendence." Merton writes in *Life and Holiness* that "the strength of this building depends on the extent to which the Holy Spirit gains possession of each person's heart, not on the extent to which our exterior conduct is organized and disciplined by an expedient system."

In the Christian tradition, church is simply people who have experienced, through the teachings of Christ, the truth of *Emmanuel* -- God among us -- and attempt to make it the center of their lives, living out its implications. In spite of the chaotic array of religious organizations claiming to be the "real thing," there are only two kinds of churches: the "institutional church" with its power structure, fundraising, and packaged curriculum; and the "holy church," which is manifested in the selfless love of individuals, both within and outside the organization, who have awakened to the reality of the living God.

The Development of Christianity

How could one of the most radical teachings on inner transformation be turned into the dreariness that goes on in most churches on Sunday mornings? The historical reasons began as far back as A.D. 312, when the emperor Constantine won a crucial battle and decided that his victory was due to the fact that he had experimented with putting crosses on his soldiers' shields. From then on, Christianity became a state religion, as opposed to a secret underground movement that brought certain death to its adherents if they were found out. Now, membership could guarantee tax write-offs.

Centuries later, the bishop of Rome decided to carve out western Europe for himself and branded it with a legalistic form of religion that has dominated our societies ever since. What was lost in the process was the Eastern form of Christianity coming out of Palestine, Syria, and Egypt. This teaching is truer to the original meaning of the Aramaic expressions spoken by the Christ to Middle Eastern people. It is more focused on the development of the inner life and has been preserved in the traditions of Eastern Orthodoxy.

In the *Philokalia,* a compilation of teachings from the third and fourth centuries, there is a gnosis on the watch of the heart and the uses of attention that is as potent a form of human transformation as can be found anywhere.

The mystics of the fourteenth century, the dawning of the Renaissance, and the upheavals of the Reformation certainly struggled against the more grotesque distortions imposed on the churches, such as the sale of indulgences. But by the time we reach the American frontier of the nineteenth century, we find a new misinterpretation, unexpectedly born out of these attempts at purification.

Biblical literalism was made possible because the "baby was thrown out with the bath water." By dropping all the wisdom developed through the centuries, from Clement of Alexandria in the second century to Meister Eckhart in the fifteenth, the preachers traveling through the new territories began to turn the Scriptures into a one-dimensional caricature, thereby overlooking the clear injunction that "the letter kills, but the spirit gives life." Gone was the allegorical method of Origen and Augustine, gone was the poetic intuitive understanding of a John of the Cross or an Ephrem the Syrian.

Suddenly, a new phenomenon was on the religious scene: bibliolatry. The book, stripped of its bottomless spiritual depths informed by Hebrew mysticism and a consciousness of the universal *Logos,* now defined life and became a weapon of separation rather than a roadmap to unity. This misuse of sacred writings was countered with the "historical critical method" which still reigns in seminaries to this day. Here, the findings of archeology, along with the application of rational and secular forms of literary criticism, are the foundation for the exegesis of Biblical texts.

Though identifying the context in which a teaching was given is certainly superior to a dull acceptance of every jot and tittle as the divine expression, we are still left with the same gaping black hole. What is the inner meaning of the teachings that has the power to transform human beings? The inability to answer this question is the source of modern churches' irrelevance to the spiritual journey.

The Potential of the Christian Way

One clue that points to the presence of life beneath the rubble of distortion that makes up the contemporary church, is found in the list of rather extraordinary individuals who understood the nature of this treasure in spite of everything. Consider this roster in our century alone: Albert Schweitzer, Nicolas Berdayev, Evelyn Underhill, Thomas Merton, C. S. Lewis, Mother Teresa, Alexander Solzhenitsyn, and Malcolm Muggeridge.

There are many others, of course, famous and unknown, who have witnessed the incredible transformation available through the teaching preserved in the church. These are people whose inner lives caught fire and metamorphosed them into radiant children of the divine spirit. Their impact on the world around them is undeniable, and the gnosis glowing within their being is as wondrous as any esoteric mystery. Each of these people discovered that the dogmas so poorly preached from the pulpits are carriers of experiential wisdom. They have developed "ears to hear and eyes to see" in spite of all the obstacles, particularly that of the church itself.

Every generation has produced such persons, and they pass on the torch in the dark night of human ignorance. This is why those who seek spiritual awakening cannot entirely disregard the church in spite of itself. It is a vessel that carries a sacred cargo, one that is known to give life to those who find it. And the most astonishing thing of all is that this secret cargo often draws the seeker to itself long before he or she has any idea that it exists.

The paradox, then, remains virtually unresolvable: Does the church as we find it in our time foster the inner life? No. Does the church hold the keys to a new consciousness? Yes. In the last few years, signs of hope have appeared concerning the church's role in the future. The influx of women into ministry, and persons who have journeyed through the holistic mindset of the New Age, promise to impact the spiritual dimensions of the church's teachings. Also, the recovery of Eastern Christianity in the West is providing us with a theology steeped in insights that are both highly pragmatic and profoundly mystical, although they are not any more generally accessible in mainstream

Orthodoxy than they are in Protestant or Catholic churches.

Furthermore, those who are on the spiritual journey need to look beyond the cobwebs of old associations that hang over the teachings of Christ. Rejecting the external trappings of a religion that seems like a rotted fruit about to fall from the tree of civilization does not imply rejecting the experience to which it originally called us: the transmutation of human consciousness through the breakthrough of divine light. The great visionary mystics of Christianity, many of whom were persecuted by their "mother" the church, offer powerful testimony to the worthiness of the teaching. Whether or not the vessel that carries this cargo is doomed to crash upon the rocks of its own failures is of little concern. The real issue is: Can a new community of enlightened persons, radiant with the humility and intimacy of the divine, who are the true marks of Christians, arise out of the ashes?

4

Cleansing the Temple
A Deeper Meaning

We have before us a text that is very well-known. In fact, most people who don't know Holy Scripture know this story. Because it is a Christ event, it is much more than just a happening in time and space. Nevertheless, it takes place in time and space. Here we are at the Passover in Jerusalem; the city has swollen from 50,000 to 180,000, with people coming in from Rome, Egypt, and from all over the known world. They are in the Court of the Gentiles, which is two football fields long. This is the place in which the teaching event occurs.

So we might wonder, "How did one man in that kind of space with thousands of people and thousands of animals, create such turmoil?" There were guards with spears and swords, and there were priests on the prowl. So the question arises: "Why did they not just stop him?" This is one of the cracks in the story where you can see through into a teaching that is eternal in its meaning and purpose. This event of buying and selling was not, in itself, some kind of terrible activity. It was holy sacred law. In Exodus 30, we find the following words: "Then the Lord said to Moses, *"When you take a census of the Israelites to count them, each one must pay the Lord a ransom for his life at the time he is counted."* "The time he is counted" means when someone turns 20 years old and joins the adult community. The Torah then reads: *"Each one who crosses over to those already counted is to give a half shekel."*

This religious obligation was fundamental to a people who were focused on remembering God in every possible way. It was not a tribute to the temple and the priesthood, but a sacrifice to the Holy One. At the Semitic origins of the word "sacrifice" is the meaning *"to approach God,"* to be enabled to come closer to that which is holy and pure, and know that we are forgiven and cleansed. All of us, deep in our hearts, are designed to want to come closer to God. And in those days, they did it the ancient way -- slitting the throat of an animal. That may seem terribly primitive to us, but it was done for the family, the community, and for the purpose of atonement.

The money changers were present because the Romans did not allow the Jews to make their own money. So they had Roman coins which were engraved with the face of a human being and with words about the emperor's deity. Hebrew ceremonial purity required that such a blasphemous coin not be used for holy purposes. So the Jews had to obtain coins from Tyre which only had numbers on them. An exchange was necessary. They were following the Law of Moses. So we must go deeper into the meaning of this event, because what happened there was not about Jesus getting angry.

What Jesus was actually doing becomes clear when we consider the priests' words when they turned to him and noticed this one man creating a scene, interrupting one of the high holy feasts. Instead of saying, "Catch that madman, surround him with spears," they later ask him: *"What sign can you show us to reveal your authority?"* They knew this had not been a moment of anger, but that it was prophetic manifestation. Throughout Hebrew history, the prophets were known to have incarnated their messages. Jeremiah walked through the streets with a yoke on his shoulders representing the burden of exile that was about to befall his people. There are many such examples, and multiple ancient prophecies were manifested that day by Jesus' actions at the Temple.

Consider Zechariah 14:21: *"And there shall no longer be traders* (merchants) *in the house of the of Lord of hosts on that day."* This was a prophecy that merchandising at the Temple would cease on the day that the Messiah would change the very nature of religion. Jesus was expressing something beyond violence and destruction, and everyone present recognized that it was a manifestation of prophecy. Consider the great Isaiah: *"I cannot endure solemn assemblies with iniquity…They have become a burden to me…Wash yourselves, make yourselves clean, remove the evil of your doings from before my eyes; cease to do evil, learn to do good."* Or the words of Hosea, *"I prefer mercy not sacrifices."*

In his actions that day, the Anointed One wasn't merely disrupting the temple ceremony; He was creating a new way -- a way that is not about external acts but internal change. From that day forth, it was no longer about "How much can I give to God to be forgiven?" but rather about having a pure heart. It is the transition to a deeper form of relationship with God, and nothing less.

We hear in other texts Jesus saying, *"You have made my house a den of robbers."* Most readers assume that he's talking about the merchants. But this is not an original quote from Jesus. It is another prophecy from Jeremiah 7: *"Will you steal and murder, commit adultery and perjury, burn incense to Baal and then come and stand before me in this house which bears my name and say we are safe, safe to do all these detestable things? Has this house which bears my name become a den of robbers to you?"* In other words, the Temple has been turned into a refuge to hide from our godless ways. To put it another way -- we come to church and all our godless actions are overlooked. This is no longer first century Jerusalem, this is up close and personal. He is saying: "Are we making the holy place a hideout where we can live a godless life as long as we show up on Sunday morning and sing a few songs?

This is, of course, the great hypocrisy of religion which so many in our time condemn Christians for, because they see only the contradictions. But followers of Christ must understand that this is the transition point where going to church is not an external activity, unrelated to how we behave on Monday morning. It is the height of all behavior from all week long, where we renew, purify, and regenerate. We join together as people of faith and strengthen each other for the journey.

The more you go into scripture the more you discover, and the more you find that there is more to be discovered. You could meditate on such a text to the end of your days and continue to find new meaning. That is the glory of the depth of Holy Scripture. So, with that in mind, let me take it a step further. The Greek verb for "driving out," used when Jesus drives out the merchants, is *"exebalen"* which is usually translated as *exorcism.* Jesus exorcises the temple of its demons. So when the priests say to him, "Show us a sign," his response is: *"Destroy this temple and in three days I will rebuild it."* This is the very statement that is used in other gospels to convict him. If you look at Mark 14, it is written, "I heard him say that...he said that." They were thinking that Jesus was going to take a donkey cart full of dynamite and park it by the Temple to blow it all up. This is the absurdity of taking these writings literally. But in this case, Jesus clearly uses different words. When he says "Destroy this temple," he uses the word *"Naos"* which means "inner sanctuary" or dwelling place of God, as opposed to *"Hiro"* which means the actual Temple complex.

So in that moment he turned the Temple of God inward rather than making reference to a building. In other words, you and I *are* the Temple of God. We are told that Jesus drives out the buyers and sellers -- what do we know about buyers and sellers? They're only interested in their profit, right? So you and I are called, through the Spirit of Christ, through the part of us that truly wants to approach God, *to drive out that part of us that wants nothing to do with God.* We are called to exorcise that part of ourselves that is content to live a godless life. That is the deeper meaning of *cleansing of the Temple.*

Another prophecy from Psalm 69:9 tells us: *"Zeal for your house has consumed me."* But if you look at the next line in that prophecy, it is amazing what you will discover: *"Zeal for your house has consumed me; and the insults of those who insult you fall on me."* In other words, the desecration of sacred things -- the desecration of God -- falls on Christ as representative of God. Now, see how this happens in your own life. You seek to do good and to follow Christ's way, and it is Christ's way -- goodness itself -- that is desecrated when your friends mock you and reject you, or when your loved one turns away from you as you seek to do good. So don't feel sorry for yourself. You are in good company.

But there is still more! We find that this revelation of prophecies is changing religion forever from an external ritual to an internal reality. We find that Christ is telling us that the real thieves in the temple are within us. What is a thief? Can we all agree that it's someone who says he possesses what is not his? So those who say "I'm very generous," but only give out what they don't need, are stealing the idea of generosity. Or, "I'm a very compassionate person, but only toward the people I like." Do you see how that works? Claiming to be what we are not, is stealing!

So on the spiritual level, *we* are the buyers and sellers in the temple who need to be cleansed by the Spirit of Christ within us, which understands that the House of God is neither a refuge nor a hideout for anything that is unholy or that is not devoted to God. So suddenly, this first century storybook is no longer about Jesus being angry. I have heard the most perverse misuse of this event when people say, "Well, Jesus got angry, so why can't I?" As though the holy anger of Christ for the honor of God, for the transformation of religion and for the fulfillment of prophecy, had anything to do with our little hissy fits, our impatience, bad attitudes and self-obsessions!

Let me prove it to you: in Matthew, right after this tsunami of an event, Jesus is healing people off in the corner, surrounded by children singing "Hosanna to the son of David." He is in such peace that children are happy to be with him. It's not about him, it's not personal. So when we deal with this anger thing, let us not turn to that scene of Jesus and say, "It's okay to be angry." The teachers of Christianity down through the ages have always said "be angry and do not sin." This holy anger means that we are to take that energy that boils up in us, which we all know only too well, and instead of letting it have its way, to focus it, discipline it, and use it to motivate ourselves to not be the buyer or seller in the temple. Let your own capacity for powerful outrage be aimed at cleansing your temple and finding out what kind of power is within you to change, to be different. Find out how much power it takes to keep one's mouth shut, to not respond to offense and all of those things that corrupt the temple of God. Make your temple a place of peace.

If you want peace in the world, *be* peace. Use your desire to honor God, use your outrage at the dishonoring of God, and use your own behavior to incarnate this teaching, and you will taste the things of the Spirit.

5

Warnings

"If any of you put a stumbling block before one of these little ones who believe in me, it would be better for you if a great millstone were hung around your neck and you were thrown into the sea. If your hand causes you to stumble, cut it off; it is better for you to enter life maimed than to have two hands and to go to hell, to the unquenchable fire. And if your foot causes you to stumble, cut it off; it is better for you to enter life lame than to have two feet and to be thrown into hell. And if your eye causes you to stumble, tear it out; it is better for you to enter the kingdom of God with one eye than to have two eyes and to be thrown into hell, where their worm never dies, and the fire is never quenched." (Mark 9: 42-48)

Be sure once again that this is not quite what it sounds like. So let's not get literal again. These mighty teachings from the Anointed One are methods, instructions, and very important, relevant words. This particular passage is filled to the brim with multiple teachings.

We begin with the strange statement from the disciple saying, *"We saw someone casting out demons."* Let me stop right there, because that shuts the mind down, doesn't it? So why don't we translate the words as: *"We saw someone doing good, someone healing in your name…but he wasn't one of us."* Now this "doing in the name" business is very significant, because in ancient times a name meant something. The name Yeshua was full of Yeshua's power and presence, it wasn't merely a word. It was received in a way that invoked that presence.

29

So "knowing the name" is powerful. And using the name meant *relationship* with that power. So the disciples are outraged that someone who is not one of them, who doesn't wear the same clothes or travel in the same group, would dare to use that name.

If good is going on, if God's word is truly expressed in love and action, then we all belong together. The glory of this particular movement is in recognizing that unity, regardless of creeds and doctrines and costumes, is the heart of the matter. In a world that is so full of conflict, dissension and rejection, let us remember that in the words of the Christ himself, we are called to acknowledge, accept and receive those who do good, those who are compassionate. This includes in the twenty-first century the Muslim, the Buddhist and Hindu, not just other Christian traditions. Wherever any human being is acting in compassion, there is the Spirit of Christ.

We like the comfort of the familiar, yet Jesus is challenging us at the deepest level. Wherever good is active, there is the Christ consciousness. It doesn't belong to a particular group, it is bigger than we are. Jesus says the flipside of that in Matthew, *"Whoever is not with me is against me. Whoever does not gather with me scatters,"* and that becomes the rest of the teaching in this section -- the scattering of our lives. We begin with this idea of those who are on the inside and those who are on the outside. Who is on the inside? The disciples of Jesus, those closest to him, and they seek to do a healing and they cannot. This is a paradigm of impotent religion.

Jesus exclaims, *"O unbelieving generation. How long must I be with you or put up with you?"* The disciples themselves cannot manifest transforming goodness as channels of blessing, but this stranger can. What then does it mean to be on the inside? What is it to understand something of this Holy Spirit, this energy of God? Clearly, it is not simply showing up at the right time to church or expressing the right belief. It is *being that goodness*, that is, being on the inside of Christ's reality even if you don't know it.

Then, suddenly he switches from that call to becoming not just believing, but to actively manifest that which he is calling us to do and to be. We come to this strange saying, *"If anyone causes these little ones to stumble."*

Little ones, *mikroi* in the Greek, is not the word for "child." It is the word for microscopic believers, or the ones who are vulnerable in their efforts to understand, to connect with Spirit, to get on the path that Christ shows. He is referring to the one who can be easily knocked off the spiritual path and fall away. Who is that one? It is each one of us. No matter how dedicated we are, it is always just a little part of us that wants to do God's will, because the vast majority of our nature wants to do our own will, have our own way, and care only for ourselves. It is human nature. So we are called to cherish that little part within us that is interested in transcended spiritual matters, and to nurture and protect it. Then, we have to listen to these mighty words: "Whoever causes that purity within a human being who is seeking God to stumble..." The word "stumble" here means "scandalize," to be scandalized -- to be so offended and upset that they give up on the journey to God.

Imagine a visitor who finally dares to come into a church after twenty or thirty years, who had given up on it and is going to try it one more time. They walk into our entrance and there you are, unwelcoming and in a bad mood, so they turn around, walk out and never come back. "Woe unto you!" says the Holy One. Then he gives us the perfect metaphor, *"It would be better if a millstone..."* The words are *"mulos onikos,"* a millstone dragged by a donkey. It's so heavy that no one can pick it up. Imagine such a stone "tied around your neck and thrown into the sea..." What is that a picture of? There is no survival. It is hopelessness. It is the end. And Jesus teaches that this is a better deal for us than causing another person to turn away from the spiritual journey. That is how serious this is.

We have a great responsibility to not be the ones who keep another from finding their way to God. And how easily we can let that happen! Christianity has been rejected by so many because of its hypocrisy, the "do what I say not what I do" attitude. We are called to live out that spirit of Christ in such a way that people will say, *"I want some of that. That's the way home."* And that is what we are called to be. So take this business seriously. You know the Master does.

He goes on to give us instructions: *If your hand or foot offends you, cut them off.* We know that the hand is not responsible, it's what is in the mind and heart that makes the hand do something. The foot may lead you on the path to mistakes and temptations, yet again, it's the mind and heart that direct it. And the eye -- *first take the beam out of your own eye; if your eye is not sound, your whole body will be full of darkness...* What is he saying here? Hand, foot, eye, what is that? It is our whole being. It's our totality -- it's all of us, it's everything we are. If there is any aspect of our personality that works against the "little one" within who is seeking to please God, that is spiritual warfare at its most fundamental.

Let's get more specific. If a bad thought enters your mind, a godless thought, a negative thought, a hateful thought, what are you to do? What does Jesus say to do? Cut it off! It works, believe me. You have to want to apply it, though. If you allow yourself to have those thoughts because you really don't care, and Jesus has told you, where does that leave you?

In Romans, Paul says, "He or she who does not have the spirit of Christ does not belong to him." We have to actively seek to have that spirit of harmony, of forgiveness, of peace. We are asked to do the drastic thing, not the bloody thing, and the drastic thing is to cut off, to stop those bad habits, the bad thinking. Most of the time we're in denial. We don't want to even see inside. But this teaching tells us that if you're going to be a follower of

Jesus, a spiritual person, you have to look within and deal with it drastically. It's not acceptable, according to the Eternal One, to think and act in the old way. It is not okay. In fact, he goes further. We have heard the words "go to hell." The word "hell" in the Greek is "Gehenna." It's not Hades, the land of the dead. It's the Hebrew "Gehenon" which means the Valley of Hinnom, and what's that about?

The Valley of Hinnom, south of Jerusalem, is where the ancient kings who threw out their faith as revealed by Moses, worshiped Pagan gods like Moloch. And how did they worship? By offering infant and child sacrifices, and by burning them on the altar, the most horrible thing imaginable. Finally, in the days of Jeremiah, King Josiah put an end to that nightmare. For centuries after that, the Valley of Hinnom was a desecrated place. It was the garbage dump of the city of Jerusalem, where fires never went out and where gruesome worms constantly gnawed at the garbage. What is that a picture of? Wasted life, total loss, nothing to be salvaged. So what is Jesus saying to us? *"If you're not gathering with me, you're scattering."* If you're not making the effort to cut off the negative thought, the godless thought and feeling, life is waste. Do you see how important it is to the Holy One? For too long Christianity has been just a thing to do on Sundays, the thing everybody does. But far more is required of us according to the Christ, and now, not many people are doing it. So we have a chance to take it seriously again and to realize that it's all inside of us, it's about who we are. Don't feed the poor and have nasty thoughts at the same time, not when he says "cut it off." Devastated life, unhappiness and brokenness are what will result if we don't live this out. We will have lost our opportunity to let God enter our lives and fill us with the joy of living and the power of love that overflows with miracle. That's the promise, that's the call, that's the way of Christ for everyone.

6

I Am with you Always

After these things Jesus showed himself again to the disciples by the Sea of Tiberias; and he showed himself in this way. Gathered there together were Simon Peter, Thomas called the Twin, Nathanael of Cana in Galilee, the sons of Zebedee, and two others of his disciples. Simon Peter said to them, "I am going fishing." They said to him, "We will go with you." They went out and got into the boat, but that night they caught nothing. Just after daybreak, Jesus stood on the beach; but the disciples did not know that it was Jesus. Jesus said to them, "Children, you have no fish, have you?" They answered him, "No." He said to them, "Cast the net to the right side of the boat, and you will find some." So they cast it, and now they were not able to haul it in because there were so many fish. That disciple whom Jesus loved said to Peter, "It is the Lord!" When Simon Peter heard that it was the Lord, he put on some clothes, for he was naked, and jumped into the sea. But the other disciples came in the boat, dragging the net full of fish, for they were not far from the land, only about a hundred yards off. When they had gone ashore, they saw a charcoal fire there, with fish on it, and bread. Jesus said to them, "Bring some of the fish that you have just caught." So Simon Peter went aboard and hauled the net ashore, full of large fish, a hundred fifty-three of them; and though there were so many, the net was not torn. Jesus said to them, "Come and have breakfast." Now none of the disciples dared to ask him, "Who are you?" because they knew it was the Lord. Jesus came and took the bread and gave it to them, and did the same with the fish. This was now the third time that Jesus appeared to the disciples after he was raised from the dead. (John 21:1-14)

We have before us so much more than a story, so much more than a sighting. It is the climax of the Gospel of John, the spiritual Gospel. We have here such mystical depth, such profound divine wisdom, that it would behoove us to enter deeply into these seemingly simple words and images and discover what eternal truth there is for us here today. Let me set the context for you: The verses right before this refer to that famous moment of those apostles in despair and fear, locked in a room, locked away from the Romans and from all those out there who wanted to hurt them. They were desperate and hopeless. In that moment of utter fear, appears the Risen Lord through the locked door, so there could be no greater spiritual, supernatural, other-worldly event than this. You remember doubting Thomas and the extraordinary gift that the Risen One gives him to touch his wounds.

After that unbelievable revelation of God's victory over darkness, over cruelty, over evil, Peter says, "I'm going to go fishing." In that holy moment, in that locked room, the Lord says, *"As the Father has sent me so I send you"* -- take this awareness, this knowledge, this new understanding and share it with the world. But Peter wants to go fishing. What does this tell us? What does this teaching reveal about the human condition? Haven't we all in some way or another had a special moment in life -- on a beach or on a mountain top -- where some illumination, some experience of peace that transcends all circumstances envelopes us? I like the translation "a peace that no one understands." Haven't we all had glimpses of that? We are designed to have those experiences. It's not for the lucky few. It's for all the children of God who awaken to this reality, who are not completely hypnotized by what passes for reality.

So we've all had these precious moments...and then we want to go fishing. We want to go back to the familiar, to the routine, to the old ways where everything's a whole lot simpler. We can't handle that much ecstasy, that much amazing grace, that call to share it with others and bring God's benediction to others. So he goes fishing. And what happens? What happens when we turn away from the call of God on our lives? When we turn from the experience of the Presence of God and go back to the familiar, to the routine, to the boring but comforting world we know so well. What happens? We don't catch anything! They fished all night and they could catch nothing. There's a great lesson in this. There is no blessing, there is no catch if we try to do it all on our own in the old familiar ways.

We're like the two-year old who says, "I'm going to do it my way." And we never seem to outgrow that, do we? They caught nothing -- barrenness. Then, the darkness begins to break, just like the Psalm says, "Weeping lasts for a night, but joy comes in the morning." The mist begins to break, the darkness is cut through with light and here comes a solitary figure, a stranger on that beach. And what does this figure say? *"Children..."* Isn't that beautiful? It's another profound teaching revealing our true identity. He says *"Children..."* That's so extraordinary that even some translations can't render it. If you look at the New Revised

Standard version it says, *"Friends, hey there!"* Not children, calling us by our true identity. This stranger continues: *"Have you caught any fish? Do you have any blessing in your life today? Are you aware of the source of blessing today?"*

Then in the next teaching, the stranger says, "Cast your net to the right." In other words, *"Don't do it that way, do it this way."* Apply the teachings: *Don't live in anger. Don't live in impatience. Don't live in unforgiveness; cast your net the other way... the way of Christ, the way of goodness, the way of unconditional love, the way of non-judgment...try it that way.* And what happens? Such a great haul, they can't lift the net up. Just like in the multiplication of loaves and fishes, that overabundance of God's grace, which is the nature of the God revealed by Jesus. So what is that teaching? What is that promise?

If we live the teachings, if we manage to obey, everything changes. The disciples don't know who this man is, but they do it anyway. Sometimes all we've got left in the midst of abandonment and hopelessness and worry and lack of faith, is obeying. "Because he said so, I will do it." So John, the intuitive one, the spiritual one says, *"It is the Lord."* He hasn't recognized him yet but he knows that this can be the only way this sort of thing happens.

In the most simple moments, the most ordinary moments of our lives, in acts of random kindness and someone's gift of goodness to us, we too can say, "It is the Lord." Because the Almighty One revealed by the Christ likes to appear in the simple things, in the seemingly ordinary, common things. Can you imagine if you spent your life saying, "It is

40

the Lord." "Look at that beautiful tree, it is the Lord." "Look at that kind person, it is the Lord." How your reality would change! How your joy of living would change.

Now we enter into the truly mystical teaching. We're told in simple words that Peter put on another garment because he was naked. Now here we learn not to read the Bible literally.

Once again, there are translations that won't print that word because that's a little weird. Peter was naked; he was stripped. Why? Because he had denied the Lord three times. We will discuss later what the three times means, but here, in Peter's moment of truth and at the height of this drama concerning his friend and master, the Messiah, with whom he had walked for three years and had recognized with his own eyes -- Peter totally and completely betrayed him, and was stripped. Do you know that feeling? That feeling of having lost your faith, having committed such a wrong or fallen off track so badly that you can't find your way back? He was naked. But he put on the garment. He put on the clothing of Christ, the helmet of salvation, the belt of truth, the breastplate of righteousness, he put on faith again and he leaped into the waters.

Now once again, we can't take it literally. What sense does it make to put on boots and a heavy cloak and jump into the water? Don't you know you're going to sink? Once again, it's symbolic. It's a teaching. Peter has hope again, and he rushes to the Lord. And then we're told that all the disciples dragged in that haul together -- that's why you want to read holy scripture slowly because here's a mighty teaching. It takes all of us together to bring in the blessings of God. We may discover them one at a time in our individuality, in our intimacy, in our private moments, but it is together that mighty things happen to the glory of God.

And so they bring in the fish --153 fish. Now do you really think that Andrew was counting, "1, 2, 3… hey, John, how many do you have?" And they wrote down the total on somebody's hand and put it in a book 30 years later? I don't think so. Some scholars down through time scratched their heads and said, "Well, in the old days they thought there were 153 species of fish." That's a good logical thing, it's all the fish in the world that we know of. Let me make it more complicated for you if I may.

The Bible didn't show up on the frontier as a magic book. We have cut it off from its roots, from its ancient Near Eastern mysticism and from the ways of the Rabbis who studied it with their Gematria. You see, in the Greek and Hebrew, there were no numbers, there were only letters. Each letter had a numerical equivalent, so one could put together these letters and numbers to create special meaning. For instance, The Holy name of Yahweh is the number 26, which adds up to 8, which stands for God. Then, 8 times 153 (the fish, representing the "catch" of humanity) equals 1,224 and that number represents the "The New Jerusalem." So to create the New Jerusalem, we have *God times bringing in all the people, which comprises Paradise, or the New Jerusalem.* It is the process of creating another world. "Paradise" is that world, represented by 1,224, and 153 represents bringing in the sons and daughters of God from out of chaos.

I just want to point out to you that this is deep. This is not simplistic, and certainly not stupid. And so next time you have a conversation with someone, you know that holy scripture is much more profound than any person can imagine and it's up to your openness to the Holy Spirit to hear what is in it for you. He counted the 153 fish as all of the children of God who could respond to the message. And however full the net was, it did not break. It was not torn. That word "torn" is *schisma* as in Schism. Schisms in the church, schisms in the congregation, representing division, separation. Yet it is an eternal promise of God, that in spite of our humanity, in spite of our absurdities, the gathered faithful will never be torn apart. Whatever scandals there are in churches, whatever unfortunate divisions, the net will not be torn.

Finally, let's bring it home to a personal point. Now, they came ashore and gathered around a charcoal fire, just like the charcoal fire Peter went to when Jesus was arrested, where he three times denied him. This time Christ asks him three times, "Do you love me?" And what is this about? This is the redemption of Peter. Where Christ once said, "You cannot follow me," now the story ends with "Follow me."

So for any one of us who thinks we've fallen so low that there is no hope, no forgiveness and no redemption, this message is for you. Just like Peter, you can come back to God, and just as the song says, "You can return to God anytime along the way." What a Lord we worship.

7

Being One

"I ask not only on behalf of these, but also on behalf of those who will believe in me through their word, that they may all be one. As you, Father, are in me and I am in you, may they also be in us, so that the world may believe that you have sent me. The glory that you have given me I have given them, so that they may be one, as we are one, I in them and you in me, that they may become completely one, so that the world may know that you have sent me and have loved them even as you have loved me. Father, I desire that those also, whom you have given me, may be with me where I am, to see my glory, which you have given me because you loved me before the foundation of the world." (John 17:20-24)

We have before us nothing less than the Holy of Holies, the final prayer of Jesus in the upper room. Truly, his last words, his ultimate purpose for each of us, his mission for humanity. This is the call on our lives, so we must understand it, because if we do not become one as he says, we become the failure of Christ's mission. We betray Christ's mission. This is serious. This is big.

It is our job to achieve this higher consciousness but we have to understand what it is and the process of achieving it. This is profoundly spiritual, profoundly mystical. When He speaks of "seeing my glory," he is not referring to supernatural things. In Greek, the word "glory" means *"making manifest to the hidden."* It means the revelation of his being, his character, who he is. To "see" means to *understand* -- we are called to understand Christ's character, Christ's own spirit, because he is our doorway into contact with, and experience of, God.

We are not called to merely worship something wonderful; we are called to *enter into that experience* -- "May they all be one as you and I are one, you in me, I in them." This is a teaching of the highest order. A teaching prayer, the living Christ praying that each of us may have this marvelous experience so that our joy may be complete, so that we may enter into his joy, so that we may be part of his purpose. Without this key teaching, how difficult it is for we pilgrims on this planet to find our way into conscious understanding and experience of the Holy One, of the Uncreated One.

Consider these mysteries that quantum physics have brought to the forefront: It was in 1929 that Hubble of the Hubble telescope came to the realization that galaxies everywhere were exploding away from each other. At the heart of it was this Big Bang idea, this extraordinary event in which there was a singularity, a oneness that could not be destroyed by billions of degrees of heat which nothing could survive. This event didn't happen in space, it *created the space in which it happened*. At the heart of our reality is Oneness. You and I are connected invisibly, at the molecular level. We are not separate beings. The cosmic Christ is asking us to enter consciously into that reality. And the failure of Christianity over and over again is to go for the separateness, the alienation, the "I'm different from

46

you" breakdown that has given us a history of blood, hate and persecution.

Atheists and others who reject Christianity make the sad mistake of pointing to history and saying, "Look at this mess; look at the crusades, the burning of the heretics," but all they are pointing to is the *lack of fulfilling Jesus' prayer*. This is not Christianity, this is the failure of Christianity! We who exist in this time have a shot at not failing. It's our turn now. We know that as far back as the New Testament days, there was already the shadow of separation. Peter and James in Jerusalem went against Paul and the new Greek converts. It was us against them...they have to do such and such to be part of us. They have to conform to our ways. Down through history we see how the East and West break up, and in 1054 we lose a thousand years, the treasure of early Christianity, when the Bishop of Rome was Pope over all, and no longer just another Bishop. As a result, we descendants of western civilization missed out on the source of the teachings.

Then, we find Luther trying to fix this thing, and he creates the Lutherans, more Lutheran than Luther, and another separation. Then came this madness of sects of all kinds of Protestants, until 1830, when someone rises up to create this movement here today, this denomination known as the Christian Church (Disciples of Christ) on the American frontier, in that spirit of American renewal saying, "How about if we just scrap all these man-made creeds that separate us and go back to that New Testament spirit, to that prayer, 'May they all be one?'" Listen to these prophetic words of Barton Stone, one of the founders who brings us back to this cosmic call for Oneness.

He says, "When should all be united? I answer, NOW; for if it be right, if it be the will of God, if it be the Christian's duty, if it be for the salvation of the world that all Christians should be one, then NOW is the acceptable time. If Christian union be right, disunion is wrong; if it be the will of God that they be one, it is opposition to his will to be divided; if it be their duty to be united, it is their sin to be disunited; if their union be the salvation of the world, their disunion is its ruin."

What beautiful renewed understanding of this prayer. But even then, by 1900 there is a break in the movement. They speak of restoration of the spirit of this teaching. And so some turn to the Bible and find that there are no musical instruments in here so there can't be any in the church! So we have the birth of the Churches of Christ breaking off from the movement toward Christian unity.

We humans are always in the momentum of separating out. This is why Jesus speaks like this: "*I do not pray for the world. I have given your words to them and the world has hated you.*" Understand this is the world of our psychological momentum to separate out, to not unify, to identify ourselves as over against others. In other words -- to totally betray the prayer, the purpose of Christ in the world. Jesus goes on to say, "*I want those you have given me to be with me where I am.*" The "*where I am*" is not a location. "Where I *am existing"* is the correct translation, the teaching. Jesus wants us to enter into his consciousness of Abba, that intimacy of relationship with the Holy One, the ineffable, the Uncreated. It doesn't get more wondrous and mysterious than this.

The path, the doorway is clear, recognizing that in living as Christ lives, in entering those teachings, we enter that relationship made known to humanity. So we are called again today to find a way to be in unity. How do we do that? We're all different. Some of us have accents, some of us don't. Some of us vote one way, some of us vote the other way. Yet none of that matters, for it is in finding that which brings us all together that we are unified. We are *united in diversity.* Our very differences reveal our unity.

Jesus brought together Peter, the extrovert, the loud mouth, the wild redhead fisherman with a quiet contemplative John for the purpose of showing us today that in our differences we come together around that common ground which makes us One, in which everything can be overlooked because we love God. We recognize in Christ the revelation of that reality, and that overcomes everything. If there are churches that are full of gossip and back stabbing, they have failed the Christ. It is our job now as community, as individuals to not live in that way, to tell the difference between the way of separation and the way of unity. We hear these words: *"My prayer is not that you take them out of the world..."* not that we be protected from the ugliness and craziness of this world, but that we be protected from the evil one who brings the separation.

Separation is demonic. Separation breaks us out of reality, of who we truly are. Separation creates all the ugliness Christ calls *the world*. The world hates unity because it means loving your enemy. It means overlooking differences for that which we have in common. It is Christ's way and it is radically different than what our culture teaches us. We have to come out of that into this place where the only true important thing is that there is a God and we are called to live in that light, different from the world around us. This can bring persecution, but again, Barton Stone gives us words of wisdom: *"They must first be united with the living stalk and receive its sapping spirit before we can ever be united with each other."*

The truth is that unity or oneness can only be spiritually acquired, it cannot be bureaucratic. It cannot be as the world does things. We have to choose between that part of us which wants separation from another, the majority of ourselves, and that little tiny part that seeks to live in God's way, in Christ's way, the way that makes us of the same family. It is that personal effort that brings about unity, that brings about the indwelling of that spirit of goodness and forgiveness which is the new humanity that Jesus came to create one person at a time.

It's your time now to make the choice, "Am I going to go with those feelings that cause separation from another or am I going to see it for what it is?" Remember Christ's prayer and go the other way, into the unknown territory, that consciousness of God's way, that God thing that nobody else wants to do. This is our work. This is the purpose of a spiritual community and nothing else. Sure, we're going to stumble, we're going to have to learn to get back up and forgive each other and work it out, but we know what the direction is -- The prayer of Jesus from His heart of hearts, *May they all be one.*

We become one, then we enter the joy of the Master, then we have a fulfilled existence, then we know the secret of life. We don't have to read any more books. It's deep in our hearts where we encounter the inner teacher, the nearness of God, the purpose of life. We become sanctified, set apart from everything in us and in life that would break us away from each other. We discover the glory of existence in the light of God.

PART II

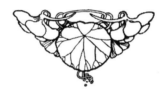

THE JOURNEY WITHIN

"The Kingdom of God is within you."

Luke 17:21

1

A Unifying Spirituality for the Twenty-First Century

This twenty-first century is bringing the human family together as never before. One of the elements that could make or break humanity's opportunities for evolution or for survival is the gatekeeper of spirituality -- religion. Will it unify us or split us further apart? There are plenty of spiritual groups in the world, but most of them reveal their exclusivity inasmuch as their members identify themselves by the motto: "I'm in the group and you're not."

Religion (which means re-linking with our Divine Source) in this new millennium must either bring us together or become obsolete. The answer to this problem is not another round of interfaith dialogue among representatives sitting in an ivory tower. What is needed is a widespread recognition of the common ground that unites all true experiences of the sacred. At the heart of nearly every spiritual teaching -- from Christian centering prayer and *hesychia* (inner tranquility) to the Sufi *zhikr* (remembrance of God) to Buddhist *mindfulness* and Hindu *advaita* (non-duality) -- there are the same elements of self-knowledge, inner struggle, inner silence, inner transformation toward compassion and loving-kindness.

These experiences cannot be captured in words with our fragmented and limited intellects. Therefore no word can be final. We can, however, use words to express our feelings of liberation from the anxieties of the ego, for the peace that transcends external circumstances, and for our devotion to something greater than ourselves. Call it Brahma, Allah, Nirvana, the God of Abraham, or the Christ, there is a Divine Presence that, when encountered, may alter the fabric of our lives. Evidence of this fact can be clearly witnessed in every century.

In this day and age, we are discarding the rationalism of an arrogant, male-driven nineteenth century and are entering into a new appreciation of intuitive awareness. Sensing the invisible in the visible, recognizing the sacred in the ordinary, and discovering the oneness of humanity is possible for us on an unprecedented scale. Now that every corner of the globe can be seen at the switch of a channel or the tap of a keyboard, we face a horizon beyond the boundaries of the past. We know in our bones that, with a little responsibility, starving children can be fed in all parts of the world. We know now that we are so connected that if the ship goes down, we all go down.

In such a world, there is no more room for the antiquated prejudice and dogmas that were shaped in the narrow confines of another age. Certainly, there are good things to inherit from the past. But everything must be measured against the most holistic and universal spiritual criteria we can perceive in our time. Such a viable spirituality for the new millennium might be described in the following way:

Authentic "enlightenment" leads to unification rather than exclusivity and fragmentation. Intolerance has no place in a healthy spirituality regardless of inherited views developed in a distant past whose subjective mores are no longer relevant to our deepest conscience. Cultural diversity can be fully embraced without fear as we accept our connections across the global family and recognize that, without embracing cooperation, survival becomes uncertain for all of us.

True spiritual leaders and teachers are recognized by the radiance of their compassion and self-transcendence. Anything less suggests that their "authority" is suspect. The written traditions and scriptures of the various religions reveal their holy wisdom when they genuinely reflect unconditional love. Ritual is valuable insofar as it enables authentic inner experience, not merely because it has always been done that way. The truth of different paths converge at the deepest levels of our being. All of life is seen as a sacrament of the Mystery that generates existence.

These fundamentals provide us with a compass for a spirituality founded on universal Truth. Anything less cannot be considered unifying, sacred, or even humane. The world has suffered long enough from restrictive religions. It is time to strip them all of their forms which separate us. If there is no compassionate light beneath them, then let them become dust in the wind.

In this new age, we can approach this formidable and all-encompassing inner work with the help of transpersonal psychology, intellectual study, emotional liberation and purification. This is the holistic development available to all of us who know that there is a special work to be done that can make cooperation among all peoples a reality in our new millennium.

It begins in the intimacy of our own psyche, as we undertake to find the "undiscovered country" of our deeper selves. In this highly individual search, we will encounter the universal aspect of our being that will enable us to bring to the world the kind of commitment and compassion that it so desperately needs.

Our experience of goodness, forgiveness, healing and transformation into the radiant persons we are meant to be is the heart and soul of a true spirituality. When individuals who are undergoing these inner experiences and yearning for more come together, a new community will be born -- one that will be open, loving and real. At the heart of such a community is authentic cooperation.

We now live in a time of smorgasbord spirituality, religion a la carte, where the lines of authority are blurred and barriers between traditions and cultures are crumbling. These are times of extraordinary possibilities in which humanity's loftiest and most powerful knowledge is being made available to anyone who yearns for it. But therein also lies the danger: one of confusion and lack of discernment. What is ultimate Truth? What is the summit of human transformation? Spirituality is meant to awaken us to this life-long becoming. It is by definition nothing less than the blossoming of human beings into children of the universe living in the light of that sacred mystery which created all things.

Ritual, holy scripture, liturgical celebrations must lead us to this state of consciousness or they are dead ends. All spiritual leaders must reflect and transmit something of that light or they are charlatans and impostors. And what is the basic characteristic of this metaphorical light? Unconditional love. To know that we are loved is the secret which religion reveals. It has no other message and no other purpose. But what power that knowledge contains! It is indeed "saving" knowledge. Kierkegaard told us: *"If there is an equality among us in which we truly resemble each other, it is that not one of us truly thinks about being loved."*

It is this "faith," this knowing which gives birth to inner freedom, confident joy, indomitable hope, and radiant love for all other beings. This is what the man from Nazareth came to tell us and it is the very simplicity of his cosmic message that got him nailed to a cross. In the light of that pure, unadulterated and overwhelming consciousness, all of the complexity, arrogance, and thirst for power found in human history down through the ages is revealed for the tragic and shameful emptiness that it is. Does the straightforward, no-nonsense core of religion mean that we can be rid of temples, fancy robes, musical instruments and all the props that go into creating a religious community? Perhaps, for all of that is only meant to assist the inner experience of awakening to a new consciousness of the divine Presence in our lives. If you can use it, if it works for you, then by all means take advantage of it. Sometimes a chapel or temple is the only place in our society where one can still find a silence enabling such an encounter. If, on the other hand, these sects and artifacts reek with negative associations, then walk away from them and find a quiet grove in the woods (if you still can).

The injustices of the world will never be changed until individuals have changed. And individuals will never change until religion as inner transformation has penetrated to the heart of their being and made them into new persons. Change happens one human being at a time. It is your transformation, my transformation, that will make a difference in this wondrous but troubled world of ours, as we become who we truly are beyond the mundane limitations of the narrow realities in which we function.

The fact is that the discoveries of quantum physics have opened new possibilities of looking at spiritual ideas in a way that overcomes paradoxes and reveals a new unity between them. Both religious persons and scientists have been guilty of creating obstacles for this new perspective. The rigidity and ignorance sanctified by dogma in the religious world on the one hand and the shocking materialistic superficiality of the scientific community on the other — even among popular scientists like Carl Sagan — have kept the debate irresolvable.

But we are living in a new time when those prejudicial boundaries can be crossed. Knowing that the atom can be split and reveal an entire universe of subatomic forces presents us with new scientific data proving that the cosmos is more mysterious and complex than we ever imagined. We have left behind the mechanistic ideas of Descartes for the world of wonder uncovered by people like Einstein, who stated, *"The most beautiful and most profound emotion we can experience is the sensation of the mystical. It is the sower of all true science. He to whom this emotion is a stranger, who can no longer wonder and stand rapt in awe, is as good as dead. To know that what is impenetrable to us really exists, manifesting itself as the highest wisdom and the most radiant beauty which our dull faculties can comprehend only in their primitive forms — this knowledge, this feeling is at the center of true religiousness."*

Bridging this seemingly infinite chasm between science and religion has brought to life again the wisdom of Christian mystics like Jacob Boheme and William Blake, who saw eternity in a grain of sand. Now there is little excuse for disregarding the link between the two and the possibility of an entirely new grasp of the meaning of "God" and the purpose of life on Earth. The alchemists of old knew this centuries ago, as did the magi and astronomer-priests of earlier civilizations for whom all of creation was sacred.

A mentality that would take us back to the Scopes trial of the first decades of the last century is an anachronism in this age and can no longer be tolerated as an acceptable argument. Spirituality and religion are particularly concerned with reality, and when science tells us that reality is more multidimensional than our senses reveal, then we are beginning to find common ground. Until recently, this deeper understanding that united the two fields was hidden in the world of esotericism and metaphysics, a subculture rejected by both mainstream religion and science. Modern developments are erasing that difference, and we are finding physicists with faith and clergy delving into the latest scientific discoveries.

From learning that the center of the expansion of the universe is everywhere, it is not a big leap to understanding the teachings asserting that Greater Mind and ultimate meaning are within each of us. When we begin to make those connections, we are on the threshold of personal transformation. In its wake comes even greater knowledge and the unification of those two old enemies, and the beginning of true cooperation across the spectrum of human thinking and activity. This unification is a liberation of the human spirit, with the power to release us from the chains of old prejudices and lead us into a new day in which the interconnectedness of all things becomes part of our daily reality. True spiritual awakening then becomes possible, and the merging of science and religion may well lead to that cooperation which is nothing less than the evolution of humankind.

2

The Power Within:
A Psychology of Inner Development

Many of us know deep in our hearts that there is more to life than paying the bills and showing up to work on time. Countless books from all over the world fill the marketplace with teachings on awakening to our higher potential. A number of these methods require that we put on robes or twist our bodies into bizarre shapes or move far from home and family. But spiritual awakening is entirely an inward matter that deals with psychological choices.

The most profound teachings tell us that there is no need for exotic travels and the appropriation of external accoutrements from other cultures. It can all happen right in your own backyard, at the heart of your ordinary every day existence. This is the place where authentic transformation can occur.

Here then are some specific methods of nourishing our spirit that can open the door to the power within regardless of your external circumstances. The first and most fundamental effort is the objective study of ourselves. Why? Because nothing real can take place until we know what we are dealing with. We cannot take for granted that we know how or why we function the way we do. If you want to operate a computer, you have to learn the software.

Human beings are complex software indeed and are rarely user friendly. So try observing yourself from a completely neutral standpoint. Do not judge what you see. Just see it. Observe your reactions, your attitudes, your moods and the many aspects of yourself that take charge from moment to moment. If you do this with sincerity and courage, not justifying every action and passing thought, a deeper dimension of yourself will begin to be nourished.

This simple effort begins the process of creating a space within you that is not completely hypnotized by external events. Though you still react to external circumstances through ingrained habit, there is now this sliver of your Self that is not pulled out of you. A new space of inner freedom is being created along with a new sense of what constitutes the self.

Another critical aspect of this observation is the study of our negative states. You'll be amazed at how much of our time is spent under the dominance of these dark moods and thoughts. You'll catch yourself grumbling about other people, feeling dejected over this or that event, complaining about the weather, resenting something somebody said. Nothing healthy can grow under the constant downpour of this acid rain within you. Eventually, you will discover that you can free yourself from such unpleasant behavior and states of mind. Step one is to turn off the leaking faucet: stop expressing negative emotions.

This effort of not manifesting such feelings is the beginning of separating yourself from them. You don't have to accept living in those dark states. You are not them. They are bad habits acquired over a lifetime. If you want healing and joy in your life, you must stop the momentum of negativity. If you want healthy nourishment, you cannot feed on such rotten states of mind.

One of the other important things to observe about negative states is how much energy they take away from us. If you are aware of yourself before and after a moment of rage, you will see very clearly how much energy has been lost in that brief moment. We only have so much energy available to us each day, and we can use it to be healed and renewed, or we can squander it thoughtlessly.

This is the beginning of clearing the path for new states and qualities of consciousness, where the spirit is regenerated and strengthened with the nourishment of another way of being in the world. So notice your thoughts before they plant themselves in your feelings and eventually manifest in your actions. Stop being asleep at the switch! Anger at a colleague or spouse can be caught before it has caused internal and external damage.

In that more rational, detached place before the feeling has caught you by the throat, you can notice why you are angry. What is it in you that is reacting that way? What is it in your colleague that has caused his or her behavior which is so disturbing? Anger can then turn into compassion, or at least into a new insight about yourself or another.

After self-observation and separation from negative states comes the next all-important practice: becoming present to the moment. Experience the moment as it is, for what it is. Becoming present grounds you in reality here and now and takes you out of the tempests of imagination and inner talking that fill the mind with so much noise. Become present not only to your surroundings, but to your body. Relax the tensions that you haven't even noticed before: In the shoulders, in the jaws, in the stomach. Begin to experience the revitalizing peace of being alive in this moment.

Those of you familiar with meditation know how helpful it is to regulate one's breathing in order to center oneself. Just breathing in and out slowly to ease the inner tensions is a powerful tool for nourishing your spirit in the moment. Learn to sit quietly for awhile. This is no luxury or idle behavior. We are so wracked with stress and worry that we can't even get back in touch with ourselves until we have managed to release ourselves from the grip of our anxieties. We rob ourselves of the very joy of living when we let ourselves fall into endless worry and nervous tension. Take time to let go of all that. This daily effort teaches us to stop or at least to step back from the constant flow of thoughts that creates reality for us. This means that most of our worrying and anxious considerations fall by the wayside and we are able to rise above the clouds of our immediate concerns to the larger picture of our existence as a whole. Sometimes, however, the flood of thoughts refuses to slow no matter what we do. Our nerves are so frayed that we cannot achieve the simple peace of looking out the window and enjoying the view without anything coming to mind. That's when you might employ the stop exercise.

In the midst of a thought or daydream, tell yourself to stop and abruptly cut short what is going on in your mind. Then relax your body and look around you, just seeing what is there. Take a vacation from the inner turmoil. So our daily practice for the inner nourishment of the spirit includes: objective observation of our selves, separation from negative states, quieting the mind, and becoming present to the moment. You will notice how these practices begin to take us out of our usual nervous tension: they keep us from mindlessly responding to everything around us by turning a portion of our attention inward and by expanding our perspective in the moment so that we begin to be more than just our self-centered, habitual mass of reactions.

If you apply these techniques regularly, and that is the key -- consistency -- you will soon find yourself living more frequently in that space of peace, of centeredness, of liberation from being victims of our automatic reactions. Then you will find that you become capable of a serenity, of an acceptance of what is, and of a surrender of selfishness that empowers you to help others as well as yourself.

That is when you begin to tap into the power within where true nourishment (the daily bread that seekers of spiritual awakening long for) becomes available. What is this daily bread? It is the spiritual empowerment that enables us to accept life as it comes, even with all its complications and the capacity to act rightly in any given situation. This developing inner power creates a free human being who is no longer entangled in his or her selfishness and constant stream of fears and desires. Such a person can journey through life in peace, with wisdom and compassion. Such a person makes the world a better place.

3

Our Spiritual Habitat

Spiritual teachers have described their experience of the habitat or environment of the soul as *cosmic consciousness, peak experience, the peace that passes all understanding, the inner light, becoming transparent to the divine.* Whatever words are used to describe it, the result of encountering this inner depth is always the same -- it enables entrance into a vaster identity and wisdom which enables right action to be manifested in the world.

We are each meant to live with serenity, joy, and compassionate outreach to the world around us. We are meant to be masters of our selves, capable of overcoming all the difficulties of life. This is our birthright, but in order to experience it we must recognize how far we are from living in this manner, why this is so, and what efforts we must make to live in such a way. This new awareness and these efforts are the process that leads us into the depths of our spiritual nature, our true habitat.

The first step along this path is to notice that we live in *different states of consciousness.* This is not as obvious as it sounds. I am not referring here to moments of happiness in contrast to times of depression, but to *a state of being* that puts us in touch with a deeper reality. Perhaps you have had moments of experiencing such a liberation that comes from these higher states of being. Moments of great joy, or

71

gratitude for being alive, or while standing before a scene of great beauty. Moments when our awareness is lifted beyond the knots and tensions of our worries and concerns and we are free to enjoy the experience of being fully grounded in the present and happy to be alive.

These are higher states of consciousness that open onto new horizons of understanding and wisdom. You may have had such experiences as children when we were less weighed down by the things that now preoccupy us. You may even have fallen for the illusion that those times of bliss and wonder are gone forever along with the other delights of childhood. But that is not the case. We are meant to dwell permanently in this habitat of the soul where higher consciousness dwells. It is possible to taste and live this joy and freedom, this inner awakening, even during rush hour, even at the office, even when circumstances around you are difficult.

In order to identify our true habitat, let's take a look at what it is *not*: our everyday state of consciousness. Teachings on this subject describe our usual condition of consciousness as a *state of sleep*. Though we all believe that we are fully conscious in every moment of our lives, the fact is that most of our existence is spent "on automatic." We are stimulus-response organisms: something happens to us and we react. We think we choose how we behave, but most often we are simply one giant knee-jerk reaction to whatever comes our way. Your child disobeys you and you get angry; you spill a drink on yourself and you're embarrassed; the red light lasts too long and you're impatient; the list is endless, from morning till night. It's the world of stress, of ups and downs, of good days and bad days, of insecurity, inconsistency, unreliability. It's the world we know so well.

If you think the word "sleep" is a strange way to describe our condition, just think back on the last time you observed someone watching television. The vacant stare, the loose jaw...we are virtually hypnotized by life around us, drawn out of ourselves and no more able to make choices than when we are in the middle of a dream. Things happen and we respond according to our programming. It is all consuming. Our first obstacle is therefore our wrong perspective on our lives. We take ourselves for granted. We believe that we are one and the same person all the time. But take a closer look and dare to be honest with yourself. When you're really hungry, the you that is hungry is in charge. When you're irritable, the you that is irritated is the boss. When you're tired, when you're excited, when you're mad, each mood and desire is in control. Where is the unity of one self in all that? Again, we function in a stimulus-response manner that takes away our capacity to be unified as individuals. *We cannot count on ourselves to be the same person from one moment to the next.* The person who decides the night before to get up early in the morning is not the one who has to turn off the alarm and roll out of bed. That person has a very different idea of what he or she wants to do.

To make matters worse, each of these impulses that claims to be the whole person is separated by blinders. They do not know each other. When we are our happy-go-lucky selves, we don't remember the mean-tempered one. Our condition of multiplicity is further complicated by the fact that we live so much of our life in imagination. Consider how much time is spent worrying about the future, or fretting over the past. Think of all the daydreaming that goes on in your head. And look at how we bounce from one thought to the next without any intentionality or purpose: someone mentions a word (like blue) and our mind takes us off on a tangent that gets more and more tangled until we no longer have any idea how we got to a certain mood or idea. So in our ordinary state of consciousness we are made of many disconnected selves, we are pulled to and fro by imagination and unintentional thoughts and yet we think we are in full control of ourselves.

Now we come to an even more fundamental problem: our essential nature, that which we truly are -- the sensitivities, the gifts, the inclinations we were born with -- is generally repressed at an early stage of our life. As we encounter the world around us, the essence of who we are becomes covered over by the development of our personality. Here again, we take for granted that our personality is who we genuinely are. But our personality is rarely related to our essence and our natural inclinations. Throughout our pre-teen, adolescent, and early adulthood years we have, both consciously and unconsciously, built up defense mechanisms to survive the pain of dealing with life. We have developed masks to protect ourselves or to manipulate others. Furthermore, we have absorbed into our idea of ourselves the images that our culture tells us are the acceptable way of being a man or a woman.

We have accumulated the imitations of our parents, our peers and our environment. In a word, we have covered over our essential nature to such an extent that we have to virtually undertake an archeological exploration in order to rediscover ourselves. In order to find the habitat of our soul, in order to live right, we have to be aligned with our real self. But there are powerful forces in the way. The greatest among them is negativity in all its forms: irritation, anger, impatience, depression, hatred, vengeance, jealousy, envy, and resentment. These are all poisons within us that cause us so much unnecessary suffering and use up so much of our energy, our life-force. We don't have to live like that! Even though it seems that everyone around us indulges in these negative forms of behavior, they are not the only way to live. Imagine how different your life would be without the constant stress of these wretched feelings.

But that entails dealing with our greatest foe: our vanity. Vanity is not merely primping in the mirror. It causes us to spend much of our life in self-interested activity, in thinking about ourselves, in having to be right, in asserting ourselves over others, in stubbing our pride over this or that. Vanity causes us to have a false idea of ourselves, a false sense of self-importance along with a perverse distortion of our attention through self-absorption. Everything becomes "me, me, me." So much grief and misery comes from this petty self-centeredness that disfigures our humanity. We are our own greatest source of suffering as long as we live in this state of sleep that is ruled by automatic behavior, a self-centered focus, negative emotions, multiple selves vying for control, and misperceptions of who we truly are.

So what is the true habitat of the soul? Clearly it is not merely a place. It is the life-force beyond our mistaken notion of ourselves that is seeking to come through us and accomplish its work of goodness in the world. It is that mysterious "presence" that can overcome solitude, meaninglessness, and despair. Moreover, not only is it always there -- deep within -- but it is seeking us more than we are seeking it. This habitat is common to us all. We are not merely separate, disconnected life forms as the senses suggest. We are all connected and rooted in the deeper life that brought us into being. This habitat is our source of hope and sanity in a world of chaos. We are a part of the greater life from which all things come, and with that awareness, we discover our real importance and purpose in the world. To become connected to inner spiritual home, which is so intimate to us and yet so much more than we are, is to come in contact with the very mystery of our existence. And the more we enter our true habitat at the center of our being, the more we are made whole and capable of caring for others.

4

Learning to Harness our Energies for a Higher Aim

The word "enthusiasm" comes from the Greek *en thos*, which means "in God." There is something about the states of excitement, passion, and eagerness that is related to a higher spiritual experience. One might even say that the intensified motivating energy is Spirit itself coming through us and enabling us to accomplish in the world. It is up to us to discern whether it is an energy that can manifest something good or is just a momentary "spike" driven by imagination or outer events.

That insight into the origin and quality of this heightened energy might also be translated into "using our powers for good." We all know that we can get wound up by all sorts of things, from football games to social events, to too much sugar and caffeine. We need to recognize when there is generated in us an energy that is truly inspirational and leading us in a new direction.

There are times when we "know that we know" deep within that we are being guided. As we get older, we know that our energy becomes more precious and we must learn to harness it for useful purposes rather than let it go to waste. In our youth, such intensified energy was enjoyed for its own sake even if it led nowhere but a momentary "high." As we mature, we need to understand how we can make right use of these opportunities to manifest something new in the world through this voltage of enthusiasm and empowerment.

Artists recognize the value of such moments as they are often the seeds for a new novel or musical score or some other birthing of a meaningful expression. We need to remember that after that generating burst of enthusiasm, there is then the long road of effort and focus to lead us to the completion of what that momentum started within us. This is where it might be helpful to recognize the dynamics of the musical octave with its notes and intervals. Spiritual teachings offer wisdom on bridging those intervals, the Mi-Fa at the beginning and the Si-Do at the end of the octave. In those times, the energy and desire fade and a new force is needed to continue on. How often have we started something with great zeal only to watch it evaporate at the first complication or obstacle. Even more frequent is that last interval when we are almost done and just cannot get the final impetus to make it to the end.

This phenomena can be observed in every kind of effort. It is necessary to begin our efforts with a strong "Do" that can sustain us through the first interval when our energies wane. Once again, we are faced with the need for intentionality, awareness, and understanding in order to accomplish the most basic tasks and requirements of life. It is important to calculate at the beginning what it is going to take to make it to the completion of our desired objectives. Enthusiasm and momentum are not enough. Ultimately, we need to turn to perseverance and commitment. This is true for so many efforts, from relationships to the spiritual journey itself.

We should not be surprised that the way our energy manifests is parallel to the musical octave. From the beginning of human wisdom, Pythagoras in ancient Greece had an extraordinary understanding of the music of the spheres, the laws of the musical octave being uncovered at the heart of reality itself. He stated: *"There is geometry in the humming of the strings. There is music in the spacings of the spheres."* An important aspect of our spiritual awakening is discovering our interconnectedness, that indeed "no man is an island," that we are not cut off from the web of life and its intricacies. We are certainly precious as individual beings in the sight of the mystery we call "God," but individuality does not preclude our existence being rooted in the cosmic tapestry. In truth, we are not as unique as we would like to imagine. Our authentic uniqueness comes from awakening to that higher consciousness within which links our selfhood to that of the Universe. Our uniqueness is not in our personality which is made up of varied factors, many of them illusory, but rather in the "image of God" within, that spiritual presence which is a conscious drop in the ocean of the Mind of the Universe. We are one with the One Who Is and therefore our manifestations are in line with the manifestations of everything in the cosmos. That includes the wonder of the musical octave in the vibrations of all that exists, including our desires and actions.

If we wish to carry our momentum and enthusiasm through a process that leads to completion, we will need to administer power boosts, or "shocks" to ourselves, as some teachings call them, at those interval times when we are tempted to give up or turn in another direction. The psychologist and spiritual teacher Maurice Nicoll describes the process in this way:

"At Do, when our original octave of rearranging furniture began, there was a certain period of energetic activity and a pleasure in doing something new. By the time we reach Mi, a reaction has set in and the work becomes tiring and tedious. Instead of thinking through problems we begin to compromise; inessential activities take the place of real work. The activity may continue, but the initial enthusiasm and the work have changed; now we just want to get the job done. Irritation sets in and even small problems are too much trouble to deal with. The octave of rearranging the living room furniture, instead of developing in a straight line, has started turning. Eventually a difficulty arises and the original objective is never accomplished. The 'shock' which allows the octave to continue to completion must come from outside. In our example, if at the point of Mi-Fa a friend calls and we talk about what we are doing and the problems we are having, the friend might give us helpful suggestions and encouragement. This could have the effect of infusing us with renewed energy and valuation of the project. This can explain why it is easier to do such a project with someone else who can give the shock at the place needed."

This insight into the "harnessing" of our enthusiasm and desire to accomplish a task offers us the potential to bring our efforts to completion and to find the delight of fulfillment. In this way, the initial joy and hope contained in our heightened energy is not lost or disappointed. We then become capable of following through with our dreams and inspirations, enabled to truly manifest our deepest yearnings in this world as a blessing to others. So take hold of the reins of your energies and enthusiasm for accomplishing something in this world and guide it to completion with intentionality, awareness, and commitment for the sake of a greater purpose.

5

The Transforming Power of Gratitude

Most of us know the story of Zacchaeus up in that sycamore tree. We learned it in Sunday school, the silly little song about it, lots of cartoon figures, yet this is a mighty teaching, divine wisdom for each of us on the transforming power of gratitude for being accepted. So take another look at this ancient teaching and discover what it is that is being offered to you. Let's begin with setting the context.

Jesus comes into Jericho. Now that's significant because Jericho, thirty miles south of Jerusalem was the city connected to the east, the lands of Palestine and the great east Persia, Asia, all of that and so all of the merchandise came through Jericho. Lots of spices and caravans, and it was in this city that we have our prototype or representation pictured in one Zacchaeus, a tax collector.

He reminds me of that word they used in France during the World War II -- "collaborator" -- with the enemy, with the invaders against his own people. That's who he was, collecting burdensome taxes from the people for the Romans, hated and reviled and considered as low as a murderer, thief or prostitute. He was totally rejected by his community but very rich, very important and very frightening because he was not just a tax collector, friend of the brutal Romans, he was chief tax collector. He got a piece of the action from all the other tax collectors.

What does that have to do with you and me? We have here the figure of somebody who is so hopelessly godless, so full evil, of self-interest, of wrong doing that you couldn't get any further from the holy and the pure. Isn't it interesting that this kind of character, the most ungodly possible, wants to see this holy man from the Galilean hill country? Why would someone who has essentially given up on being incorporated into the community, into the religion of his ancestors, want to see the prophet from Nazareth?

Someone who is rejected by religious people, who is so lost, who is not worth saving, somehow senses that there is something different about this new and mighty prophet. Don't you know that we are all like Zacchaeus, hopelessly lost in our imperfections? We are all in that boat and yet something about this revelation of divine compassion through the Anointed One tells us that we're accepted anyway.

Now it's no longer about Zacchaeus, it's about you. You are accepted in your limitations, in your imperfections, in your mistakes, in your sinfulness. In spite of everything, the Uncreated One has come for you, loves you, is looking for you. Is there any greater reason to be grateful?

This is our story. And what do we find here? Zacchaeus has to struggle through the crowd. He cannot get to experience, to see, to understand that which is holy without doing so. Once again, we have these obstacles to overcome.

Not only our internal ones -- our own selfishness and lack of desire to be compassionate and merciful to believe in something greater than ourselves -- but our whole culture interferes with such a spiritual effort. Some churches interfere with seeing Jesus as well. You could be rationalistic about it and say okay, he's a short guy. He's got to climb high to see, or you could make it real, personal, spiritual: All of us are short, small when it comes to understanding the deep things of spirit, in attempting to grasp what this God idea is and how to live it out. All of us are shortsighted. All of us are limited. And so he climbs the tree, and in the Middle East to this day, it is unseemly and undignified for a man of means to be seen running.

Here is this wealthiest man in town, covered in jewels, doing that undignified thing of climbing a tree. What does that tell us? He is desperate. He will do anything. He will endure mockery. He doesn't care what the hundreds of people who already hate him are going to think. Sometimes you have to not care what people think in order to "see" or understand a new spiritual perspective. It takes courage.

So he's up in that tree. This man -- rejected by all for good reasons. The righteous people have good reason to find this man unworthy. What happens? Jesus comes by and calls out: "Zacchaeus!" How did Jesus know his name? This teaching tell us that he knows your name. God knows your name. You may not know God but God knows your name. That's a shocking revelation. Nobody in the crowd whispered it to him. Jesus knows that child of God and knows you as child of God.

He tells him to come down from that tree: "I must go to your house today." The Greek word means *"it is necessary for me to go to your house today."* And what does that mean? He didn't come through Jericho by accident. He didn't run into Zaccheus by mistake, by coincidence. Rather, this is a timeless moment in which humanity is taught for all time why we ought to live in gratitude. This event *had* to be. This was designed so that you, in this time, can understand what the revelation is -- that the Holy has come for you too, whatever your limitations are. *I must come to your home today*. You, the last person imaginable.

This is an example of the divine way: God accepts us and we change. The human way is: "You'd better say you're sorry and then maybe I'll forgive you." We don't accept until we get proper repentance. In the divine way, God loves and accepts us, and we respond because we are so filled with awe and gratitude to know that we are loved by the Heart of the Universe in spite of everything.

And what happens in this wonderful revelation that ought to bring joy and gratitude to every human being? People mutter, people grumble because they are unhappy with God's goodness. So Jesus comes to the house of the one man in town that a Holy Man would never go to in order to reveal divine love. Zaccheus welcomes him gladly. That is the teaching: Welcoming such unconditional love gladly, not merely into your home but into your heart. You cannot be grateful intellectually or philosophically. You've got to open your life, your soul, your psychology, your heart to the reality of Spirit, welcoming gladly that consciousness of acceptance and love.

Zacchaeus is so overwhelmed by this love of God manifested through the mercy and acceptance of the Anointed One in spite of everything he's done, that right then and there he becomes a different person. He gives half of his wealth away to whomever he has cheated. He gives four hundred fold. In the Torah, the sacred law, the Rabbis say that if you cheated somebody, you pay them back the restitution plus twenty percent. But this man – this every person who becomes aware of such Truth -- is so grateful that he gives back four hundred percent, not to look good but because his heart is so full. Then Jesus proclaims: "Today salvation has come to this house!"

In the midst of such transforming gratitude, the Anointed One gives us his mission statement: "For the Son of Man has come to seek and save the lost." He has come to seek out each of us in our lostness, in our mistakes, in our foolishness, in our bad temper, in our pettiness. He has come to seek us where we are and to wake us up to our Creator's love and acceptance, calling us out of that lostness into a gratefulness that is conscious of the Presence of God and empowers us to authentic transformation into our true potential. Such is the power of gratitude for the sacredness of Life and its full acceptance and embracing of each one of us as a beloved child of the universe.

6

Living with Intention

"So then, let us not fall asleep as others do, but let us keep awake."
(1 Thessalonians 5:6)

"If you do follow your bliss you put yourself on a kind of track that has been there all the while, waiting for you, and the life that you ought to be living is the one you are living. When you can see that, you begin to meet people who are in your field of bliss, and they open doors to you. I say, follow your bliss and don't be afraid, and doors will open where you didn't know they were going to be."

Joseph Campbell

Certain teachings of perennial wisdom have stated that when we live without direction, purpose, or consciousness, we are under the "Law of Accident," meaning that anything can happen randomly and chaotically. They further suggest that, in increasing our conscious presence to the moments of our lives – and therefore filling them with, at the very least, *the intention of being present to our lives and true to our selves* – we then come under the "Law of Fate" where destiny and mysterious design come into play.

This should not be seen as some strange esoteric perspective. Our common sense tells us that if we are distracted or lost in imagination and fail to look both ways as we cross the street, the odds are greatly increased that an accident may occur that need not happen. So this business of "intention" is truly a cornerstone for our lives, both in its long-term direction and in our daily welfare.

World religions have made it a crucial ritual, beginning all intentional activity with spiritual invocation. The Kabbalah speaks of the notion of *kavana* as a central focus in which the practitioner commits to full engagement in what they are about to undertake. Christians, at least those still linked to earlier traditions where the numinous was tangibly present to them, may begin an intention with: "In the Name of the Father, and the Son, and the Holy Spirit." Muslims, in keeping with the spiritual depths of their teachings, may say *"Bismillah ir-Rahman ir-Rahim"* (In the Name of God, the Merciful, the Compassionate). Such invocation empowers the intention and generates a momentum that will carry the committed person a good ways toward their aim.

Unfortunately, we all know – both in ourselves and others – that such well-intentioned beginnings often wind down and sputter to a dead stop long before their goals are accomplished. It is likely that the majority of people have trouble with this phenomenon. They begin a project or job or relationship with great enthusiasm, and before too long begin to lose interest, the excitement of the new fades away, and they find themselves falling into mediocrity and eventually complete disregard of that which once stirred their hearts and minds. Most employers have witnessed such behavior and suffered the consequences.

This fact takes us back to the quote by Joseph Campbell. Commitment to intention needs to be fueled by a passion and love of the activity, project, or dream that has taken hold of us. His famous phrase *"follow your bliss"* is not a call to hedonism but a cosmic secret to true perseverance and accomplishment. For Campbell, those three words summarized the fundamental meaning of all the great mythologies of humanity. They call us to uncover and live out what is our heart's deepest yearning. For in doing so, we not only discover our true purpose in life, we unveil our identity and the destiny that beckons us onward toward ultimate fulfillment.

Becoming people guided by intention opens onto much more than the accomplishment of goals and objectives. Intentional living is a way of being. In Buddhist teaching, it is called "mindfulness," which a teacher has described in this way: *"We simply accept whatever arises. We observe it mindfully. We notice it arising, passing through us, and ceasing to exist."* In Christian spirituality it is known as "recollection," of which Teresa of Avila tells us: *"It is called recollection because the soul collects together all the faculties and enters within itself to be with God."* In some esoteric teachings, the term is "self-remembering." One definition of this last term is offered by Rebecca Nottingham in her book *The Fourth Way and Esoteric Christianity*:

Self-Remembering is making an effort to recollect what your essential Being is, your Real I. It is a paradoxical experience in that you feel your nothingness and your uniqueness, and you also feel connected to all of Creation, an integral part of all that is. In a full state of Self-Remembering, Real I is present. You can reach up to this higher state in your consciousness of Self-Remembering and sometimes touch what you are reaching for briefly. This is so that you can know and verify that this higher state exists within you. It is through your personal Work that you can develop the ability to Remember yourself in the full sense and become your Real I.

Such insight suggests that intentionality is actually the first step toward authentic spiritual awakening and the discovery of new horizons of understanding and wisdom. Intentionality is that baby step that "opens the doors of perception." It requires an effort of sustained attention and commitment which is rare in our time, as our minds are distracted and reshaped by the rapid-fire stimulus of media through every possible venue. We are each responsible for reining in our attention, taking command of this power of focused awareness, and purposefully choosing how we will live the moments of our lives. We can waste and dissipate them, like "leaking cisterns that can hold no water" as the prophet Jeremiah said in ancient times, or we can center ourselves intentionally and live fully in the present moment which then opens a meaningful path into the future, even when our plans are not entirely clear. Intentionality calls forth the best of our human nature and all its potential. It all begins with a *decision* to live in such a way, a decision that we refuse to betray. We then become useful to the universe and to our fellow human beings. That is how bliss enters our lives.

PART III

DEEP WATERS

1

A New Relationship between Science and Religion

Most of us have grown up hearing about the Scopes trial, the so-called Monkey Trial made famous by the play and later the movie *Inherit the Wind*. We know that in the Middle Ages, the Church repressed the likes of Galileo and other early scientists of Western civilization. Aggravated by the fundamentalism and bibliolatry of frontier America, which was devoid of the rich legacy of the great spiritual teachers of the past, it seems that the conflict between science and religion has always been a given.

There are certain presuppositions about the ancient Scriptures known as the Bible that have unnecessarily gotten in the way of merging the best of scientific learning and religious intuition. Perhaps the first matter to resolve is the controversy between creationism and evolution. The simple fact is that the five-thousand-year-old story of Adam and Eve was born out of ancient Near Eastern mythology that was meant to convey so much more than merely the literal interpretation of the story, which in many ways makes nonsense of the profound symbolism and wisdom buried in the imagery.

The realization that these colorful stories and their accompanying rituals were the very heartbeat of complex and sophisticated civilizations has led to numerous theories on the purpose, meaning, and value of what the Greeks came to identify as *mythos* ("the tale told"). With this definition, however, myth was reduced to the impotent state of imaginative fabrication, the pastime of simplistic, primitive minds. Yet the mythical dramas and festivals of Mesopotamian culture were concerned with realities with unfathomable depths. They were designed to exercise a vivid effect on the individual worshiper's experience.

Myth was originally expressed in a religious atmosphere that sparked the manifestation of its true intent. A spiritual experience, one that impacted the receiver to the core of his or her being, was the fundamental purpose of the myth and its accompanying ceremonies. The consciousness of the cosmos so vibrant in the earliest mythic tales of humanity is unavailable to us unless we approach it, according to the noted scholar Stanley N. Kramer, "uncontaminated by the current scientific approach and analytic mentality, and therefore open and prone to profound cosmic insights which are veiled to modern thinking man with his inhibiting definitions and impassive, soulless logic."

Christianity adopted the Torah (the Old Testament) in order to remain linked with its Jewish heritage and the messianic hopes of the "chosen people." Over the centuries, it seems to have completely forgotten about the teachings of the Talmud and the Kabbalah, which reveal the deep mysticism at the heart of these stories. For modern persons to assume that the tale of creation can only be understood from that one-dimensional perspective is to make a mockery of these revered writings.

The Scriptures contain more than surface meaning or they wouldn't deserve the name of Holy Scripture. Despite the witness of the great visionaries of Christianity, from Meister Eckhart to Thomas Merton, the general population (Christian or otherwise) has assumed this either/or mentality to the great detriment of the spiritual development of the species. In this century, some have come close to merging the best of these seemingly separate fields. The French priest-scientist Pierre Teilhard de Chardin is perhaps the most shining example of this kind of holistic understanding.

2

The Future of Religion

Down from the ages we can see clearly history teaches us that religions are transitory teachings. Wisdom has a lifespan. We are two thousand years into the life of Christianity and we know that, from very early on, the form of the church kept changing and crystallizing on and off in strange directions.

Consider the first thousand years, coming out of the Middle East, creating the Desert Fathers and Mothers who were the heart and soul of the Eastern Orthodox Church. Then in 1054 the Bishop of Rome split off the western churches and the eastern churches to go in their separate directions, with all the earliest traditions being unavailable to the west for centuries.

Western civilization arises under the Catholic Church -- Catholic meaning universal, and we know it wasn't universal because it cut out the East with the origin of teachings. Then comes the Reformation in the 1500s and we find another major break. We know that Luther was never trying to start a new church. He was trying to reform the only church he knew.

Luther was not a Lutheran, and yet the Lutheran Church began, along with all the sects that broke out from there, until today the Church Universal is like a shattered vase, with no reference to the original teachings or to the wisdom of those who were the great leaders of the faith, saints who had experience of Spirit. Now, anything goes. The Mormons create a new religion completely unconnected with the origins, with their own book "found" in the 1800s. Millions believe that the Bible can only be taken literally, when never before in history was it read that way by any of the great teachers of the Faith.

In the twenty-first century, anyone with real education and scientific understanding can find connections to the teachings of the Cosmic Christ. Certain kinds of expressions of Christianity, clearly those who take literally seven days of creation, cannot speak to quantum physics and vice versa. Many of those who have a heart for finding Truth or a sense of the Sacred cannot turn to Christianity.

Finding the wealth of timeless wisdom teachings is almost impossible when these are often unknown to leaders of the church. Many have reduced writings on holiness to a "social gospel" in order to try to find some of kind of reference point that makes sense to them. But these are half-truths. Something of ultimate and transforming significance is missing. Uncertainty and confusion are the order of the day and it is understandable that seekers, those who hunger for righteousness as Jesus says, just shake their heads and walk away. The churches that used to be the cornerstone of society are dying, disintegrating, becoming irrelevant to today's world.

We can understand that if church is seen only from the perspective of one of those broken pieces with its half-truths, then it communicates a version of Christianity that is unacceptable to the wider world. If you're one of those who hungers for meaning, who needs to find connection with the deeper Self, with Holy Spirit, you know that materialism cannot offer solutions.

Today I reach out to you and say, don't give up. Keep seeking. There is a cosmic truth to the teachings of Jesus – "Seek and you will find." You will be led to that which will care for your soul in spite of the odds being against you, and in spite of churches that are full of judgment and intolerance, who live for the sake of form and tradition rather than for experience of Spirit.

There will be plenty of crevices, traps and dead ends. Keep looking because what you are seeking for is in fact within you, and it will lead you to something that feeds your soul. Purity of motives -- to be good, to be the best you can be, to love God, will keep you safe in that search, because in many ways churches are vessels that carry a content they know nothing about.

In other words, you can come into a church -- a Catholic Church, a Protestant Church, an Orthodox Church -- and beyond the surface there is something that perhaps most of the people don't know about. You can enter into times of prayer, peace and silence, and worship that is meaningful to you in spite of the people in the church not behaving as Christians.

There is catastrophe in the Body of Christ because this is a time of loss and confusion, and a lack of authentic spiritual leadership. Don't let that get in the way of your search for a path, because no matter what human beings do in terms of making a mess of things, they cannot overcome the efforts of those who can respond or see.

There was a time when one of the military leaders, who was supposed to be a religious man, infamously said: "Kill them all and God will recognize his own!" Yet, even in times of great darkness, there arise individuals to rebuild God's church, to renew the truth of the Gospel, the teachings of Christ, the way of life made known to us in Christ. Every century, every generation has this kind of renewal that gives people a chance to reconnect with what is real about spiritual teachings.

The future of religion is truly up in the air now that we're in a global world where eastern teachings, esotericism and everything else is available. People pick and choose like a smorgasbord, a big buffet of spiritual choices. Certainly they're not going to go to their grandparent's church, they're going to seek that which speaks to them now, which touches them in ways that other forms cannot.

In this time period, Christianity has to renew itself and offer to each of us something that truly enables us to wake up. From the call of God will come conscious people who are capable of transcending themselves and bringing compassion into the world. True spiritual teaching lifts us out of sleepwalking through life and allows us to live differently even if our circumstances remain the same.

Resurrection itself assures us a path, so look beyond the form, even the forms that clearly died long ago and still don't know it, look beyond to that which is alive and well. Don't give up. It's here with us, awaiting our determinative decisions.

3

Rediscovering Christianity

There is so much baggage associated with this religion. It has been so misrepresented in the media around us, during our time and in the centuries before us. Many people point to the horrors and bloodshed committed in the name of religion, and so they throw the baby out with the bath water and disregard the content, the power within these teachings because of what human beings have made of them.

Despite the institutions, abuse of power and distortions, it is amazing that the wisdom, the life transforming power within Christianity is still available, is still around after 2000 years. There was trouble and confusion at the very beginning, going back to the church in Jerusalem, to the struggle between Peter and Paul, when they thought that it was only for them, only for their people.

The universal, eternal teaching of truth, wisdom, and revelation made known by the Christ, by the Anointed One, by one whose intimate relationship with that which is at the heart of the universe, made all the difference in the world for those who could grasp what was offered. So I challenge you, in this world of chaos and brokenness, to reconsider from a whole new perspective what it might mean to be called a "Christian." As you may know, the word "Christian" was applied by outsiders to those who followed the way of Christ and simply called themselves "the People of the Way."

To put this experience in modern language, it was a new way of living, a new way of being, a new way of understanding the world, and a new quality of consciousness. In fact much of the dogma of the church, as Evelyn Underhill, the great scholar of mystical Christianity has put it, is just a poor attempt *to express, experience.* The whole mystery of the Trinity came out from Gregory of Nazanzium seeking to poignantly express his own personal experience of wonder.

It is up to each of us to taste and see, to rediscover for ourselves what is really here. We have to put aside the devastating misrepresentations of history, the absurdities that have created layers and layers of misunderstanding and contradictions in what was originally illumination, light and joy.

Imagine a teaching that speaks of the mystery at the heart of creation as "Abba," as Daddy, with an intimacy and self-surrender that are beyond our normal human ways.

Such wisdom teachings offer unconditional love incarnated in the world. Christianity was never meant to be an exclusive, over-against type of religion. It is in fact the apex of human intuition. It is the ultimate expression of that transformation, that potential within each of us to be our spiritual selves, awakened to the Sacred, and channels of blessing to the world.

Perhaps you've known that kind of people with light in their eyes, that kind of astonishing love that heals and renews other lives because of their own love of that which is holy. In this twenty-first century, we have lost touch, not only with the roots of this teaching, but with the very sense of the sacred and the holy. We have reduced our reality to the most mundane and superficial sense-based three-dimensional box. We have made unimportant that which is the very source of our life. We have lost sight of the invisible within the visible.

So I urge you not to just throw it out because of what you see on television, because of the fragmentation of religious sects that have created multiple and superficial religions. Don't you know that in the ancient writings of the Hebrew people was profound mystical symbolism, that the number seven represented the perfection of God, that there never was that artificially set up contradiction between spirituality and science?

The scriptures were never meant to be read on the surface, and the literal interpretation was never the teaching over the centuries. It comes out of extraordinary ignorance and disconnection with the whole legacy of Christianity. The great teachers of the faith spoke of the kind of spiritual preparation necessary to approach this teaching so that intuition and openness to the inspiration of Spirit would be part of our experience. There was a recognition of the difference between the Old and New Testaments. As Jesus says: "You have heard it said, but I say to you... something new."

Some new revelation of the nature of God was presented. We can't throw it all together with the wrathful, jealous God of primitive times, of the early part of the Old Testament, and the one revealed by Jesus. Something dramatically different has taken place, and yet some have thrown it all together as one, confusing everybody.

Take the time to look into these matters and to rediscover for yourself so that it isn't stolen from you. Have the integrity to find out what it really says, what is really taught, what Meister Eckhart of the fourteenth century had to say about it. What Teresa of Avila and John of the Cross understood, what Isaac the Syrian in the ancient times, and the Desert Fathers, or Thomas Merton in the twentieth century had to say. So many haters of this religion only understand it in its most absurd level, only take some fundamentalist view and assume it's Christianity then criticize it. What a lack of integrity that is. They claim intelligence and yet they won't use their own minds to really understand and incorporate what it is that is presented here. And so in this day and age when it is so necessary to rediscover the depths, the meaning and purpose in our lives, let's re-examine what this is all about. Let's go beyond the Roman version of the West and see what the East teaches and its idea of theosis and divinization, or God realization. The ancient teachings were so much more dynamic in their theology and wisdom.

We in the West have been cut off from that for so long. Now, as we enter into a global community, all becomes available, and Christianity may recover some holistic dimension. So we find that we are not just children of the American frontier version or of the European version, but of the very origins. And then you will find that there is a mighty power, a non-exclusive, universal and eternal dimension that actually can change your psychology, your joy of life, can lift you up, can give you a sense of self beyond anything you imagined, to empower you to become truly that child of the universe, that child of God through whom miracles of goodness can flow. Take the time to seek. Take the time to rediscover the depths of these teachings and everything will change.

4

The Practice of Nepsis

These inner teachings of Christianity were preserved in monasteries, as they were instructions to monks on inner warfare, on internal self-awareness, on ascetical efforts, efforts of spiritual discipline for their own development, their own awakening to spiritual reality. This was never meant to be for the few or for a specially called-out people, or people with a particular vocation, this is for all people. And this science of spiritual development is one that is available to humanity, not merely to those who have special access to this material. As I have mentioned to you before, the split between the East and the West in 1054, between the Orthodox in the Catholic churches, in many ways cut us off from these profound wisdom treasures that are as valid today as they were in the fourth, the sixth, and the tenth centuries.

So, let's take a look at some of these marvelous gifts to humanity that have come down so hidden, though they were not meant to be. One of them is known as "The Watch of the Heart" (also known as "nepsis" in Greek). The early fathers and mothers of Christianity use this as a central method to help people unify themselves around the consciousness of the divine. The watch of the heart translates as self-observation -- observation of what is going on within us. That is to say, instead of taking for granted every thought and emotion that comes in and calling it "ourselves," allowing it to take over for the moment it's there and cause all sorts of random havoc, we must become not just vigilant, but discerning as to what is happening.

For instance, if a thought comes in that has a dark quality to it that is negative and violent, instead of making it our identity in that instant, we reject it. There is a graphic expression of this methodology in the ancient writings which says: *When the snake is coming in through the hole under the door*, that is, when the thought is about to enter your heart, to take you over and cause you to act out -- *you must cut off the head of the snake right at the beginning.*

This forceful teaching understood very clearly that if we allow an emotional thought to come in unguarded and enter our minds and hearts and "ascent" to it as they say -- agree with it, accept it, receive it -- then we become captives of it. So the suggestion which initially appears to us is assented to, we become captive to it, and we act out its wrongful expression, its sinfulness. So they perceived that what happens to you and me today is a fundamental universal human phenomenon. Something comes in to our mind, we mull it over, we let it enter into our heart, we bond with it, and then we *become* it.

Most of you know that we often suddenly get a piece of music in our heads out of nowhere, we can't even trace where it came from and it is just stuck there. The same is true with many thoughts and emotions -- sometimes we pick them up like a radio station from the environment. Think of how you feel after watching a violent movie or a horror movie. Those negative elements of fear, violence, tensions or anguish fill us and we need to be cleansed from them. So this teaching is very much a contemporary recognition of the human condition, of our condition. Jesus says loud and clear, "We must cleanse the inside of the cup," meaning our inner life, our psychological life, our spiritual life. We cannot go around with heavy negative thoughts and think that we are going to progress anywhere in the spiritual life or please God in any way. We certainly can't call ourselves religious people if we live like that, in any old way, in the darkest part of ourselves.

This is spiritual warfare -- to lift our souls out of that which seems to constantly try to drag us down. In many ways, the world around us, our culture, seems to actively, aggressively seek to drag us into the lowest common denominator, and it is up to each one of us to use our free will -- to not go that way, but go the other way. We're not speaking merely of morality; we're talking about purity of heart.

Purification is a key spiritual concept that we find down through the ages and it begins with a simple thing -- of attention, of inner attention, of developing some kind of self-awareness and self-control that allows us to not be victimized continuously by whatever is going on around us. Wouldn't it be wonderful if you could control yourself in such a way that throughout the day you remained consistent, constant in your state of mind and in what it is you'd like to be, regardless of what happens around you, even a car wreck, and regardless of anything that contributes to the chaos that takes place within.

Sometimes it's as simple as waiting in line at a grocery store that causes impatience and stimulates the adrenal glands and all that generates a state of mind that is far removed from spirit. This is a daily work, and the great genius of the early teachers of Christianity, was that they combined this vigilant attention, moment to moment, with prayer.

Attention and prayer must become one, so that more and more, and in each moment we are conscious of the presence of God. We are in tune, in touch, invoking and enabling spirit to work in our lives. That is truly the pearl of great price; truly a legacy for all people who seek that higher life which gives meaning and purpose to all that we are, all that we do, and that enables us to see the invisible in the visible, to become part of God's mission in the world, finding the true purpose for our lives.

May you become self aware, attentive and discerning, and free yourself from that which would trap you, captivate you and pull you down into the darkness. There is help! You can find it if you honestly, with pure motives, seek to live this discipline out. You will find your way to the Way -- the Way of Christ, the way of self-surrender, the way of consciousness of God, the way of the Presence of God in every moment. May you find this great gift to humanity, this revelation of truth and wisdom.

5

True Spiritual Community

Consider that strange phenomenon that we find in so many churches, so many spiritual organizations, so many places people go to leave behind that which is so human and full of conflict and negativity, searching for a refuge, a place of hope and an oasis of peace, something that offers wisdom and the input of those teachings we call religious or spiritual.

Now more than ever, people are hungering for such places, such communities, such opportunities to re-link -- which is the meaning of the word "religion"-- to reconnect with that spiritual dimension of life that offers us access to the sacred, the Holy, to our own deeper identity, to sources of empowerment for our journey through life, to help us transcend the hardship of existence and serve it with an outlook that is cleansed of selfish interests and pursuits.

And yet, when people enter churches, commit themselves to the worship life, fellowship, service, all of that which is offered in these places, they typically find that these organizations, these communities are full of strife just like any other average human operation. For many people this is disheartening and they find themselves embittered, having to leave it, giving up hope on finding such a place.

This is not the way it is meant to be, and even though we have to struggle with our human ways, our old habits, our unpleasant issues and so forth, a church which claims to be the incarnation of the Body of Christ on earth, the continuance of Christ's presence and mission, must have something different going on, must hold its members accountable for their behavior.

I cannot tell you how many horror stories I have heard over the decades of the mistreatment of clergy, the mistreatment of each other, and the toxic atmosphere generated in these places, which are meant to be the *alternative* to the conflict and ugliness of human life. There are reasons why this happens and there are ways to make it different. Just because the majority of these places are in this condition does not mean it is impossible to strive for something different.

Church is a place where something else is available, is going on, where people are *in process* -- seeking to find renewal and healing and change. Strangely enough, for many people, church is not a place of transformation. The idea doesn't even come up, but in this day and age it cannot remain that way.

The world needs such places, and if churches are not able to be environments of change and betterment, of spiritual awakening, then they have reached the end of their life cycle, they have lost their purpose and force. To reduce church to nothing more than a social agency is to betray the heart of the matter, because it is precisely out of our spiritual awakening, out of our new relationship with life, with God, and with each other, that we serve the world.

It isn't the other way around, and to turn a church into the United Way or some other social activity is to lose sight of what it must first and foremost offer, and that is the path to God, the path to encountering one's own spirit, enabling one to become the person, the awakened child of God that he or she is meant to be. Out of that transformation, people can find all sorts of ways of serving the world, even in the most simple act of random kindness.

So it is really a cop out, if not a betrayal, to reduce church to just a certain kind of servicing of the needy, without that dimension of spirit, which is its fundamental corner stone. One of the reasons this has happened is that there is a real lack of spiritual leadership in the clergy. Yet seminaries themselves often do not bring that leadership to the fore, and do not direct people to the deep waters of the faith. Many ministers have to find it on their own after seminary.

Communities are left barren, with no real guidance. Also, we know that in many cases churches have become social clubs, often inbred, unhappy narrow-minded social clubs which really need to disappear with the folks that have reduced the organization to their own private club. These places are toxic with power struggles and elders who claim that power because they have been there forever, or give more money than others. Imagine that -- an elder of the church – a reference to those saintly people who have matured on the Christian path, being reduced to a power struggle among people who are completely secular, completely devoid of any spiritual wisdom, truly ungodly.

This is blasphemy, this is apostasy, this is letting everyone down and failing Christ's purpose for all those who truly hunger and thirst for direction.

My purpose here is to help you not to give up, and to encourage you to keep searching. It is said that when times are truly dark, as these times are, when lights have gone out and the culture has become a secular environment, often full of violence, a culture of death some call it -- it is in those times of intense darkness that a ray of light can shine brightest. It can be found by those who are seeking, but one must be seeking for it. I would remind you of those marvelous, timeless words from the Gospel of John, that the darkness sought to overcome the light, but it could not, it cannot overcome it.

So even where in the church itself Christians are hiding that light or burying it alive in the misbehavior of the people, the misuse of what church is, it nevertheless can still be found. Down through this history, there have been countless stories of individuals who have been persecuted by the church, and many bright people today look at history and say, *how can Christianity offer anything after such an awful impact on history, after the crusades and wars and burning of heretics?*

But we all know that this is also a lack of integrity, because it deals with that external thing called religion and not the internal truths, the wisdom that is brought to humanity that molds and shapes a person into a being of compassion and love, which is of course the only purpose of Christ's teachings. All the rest is what human beings have made of it, so this is all the more reason to be truthful about the matter, to recognize that churches cannot be places of toxic behavior, of mean-spiritedness, back stabbing and gossip. Christians must be held accountable, and spiritual leaders must truly be spiritual people so that in this day and age an environment can be created where people can find something new, something renewing, something different. I urge you to keep searching. You will find what you seek, because spirit will lead you to it, and even though there is much disappointment and much chaos out there, eventually you will be led into those rare places where something different is happening, where priority is given to a way of being, a way of life, a way of loving-kindness which is the way of Christ; a place where people are being sensitized and made self-aware and gentler, so that in the combined community we have truly a body of people joining together for that common purpose of awakening to spirit, of loving their Creator, and of making a difference in this world.

I invite you to find out for yourself, to search for a community that is committed to this kind of renewal of humanity, re-building of church, and of authentic spiritual living.

6

The Inner Teaching

The inner meaning of the teachings of Christianity is a form of the religion that is little known to the world. You may know Christianity through the externals of what you see on television, what you see going on in churches -- the rituals, the traditions, what you grew up with -- all of these are the surface of a religion that goes back two thousand years.

Religion means to re-link, to reconnect us with Spirit. There is a saying from a profound spiritual man of our century, a priest from Belgium, that Jesus did not come to bring us a new religion. He came to put us directly in touch, in an intimate, personal way, with the spirit of God, with the Holy Spirit, that higher power from which we come, which made us, created us, and knew us before we were born. It is that Spirit which lifts us beyond the animal world of senses into the true dignity of being human. If that is troubling to you as a rational person of the twenty-first century, consider this: Our thoughts and emotions are invisible; if you look at someone from the outside, you have no idea what is going on inside. Sometimes, we ourselves don't know what is going on inside of us. Our true identity is in our psychological, spiritual selves.

And yet people identify themselves according to the surface, so this mystery of who we are is what Jesus comes to unveil, that is what makes him a revealer of Truth -- that we are children of the Holy One, not just of our earthly parents. Our potential is so much greater than we might imagine. Our opportunity for peace and joy, happiness, fulfillment -- all that we yearn for is possible in a way that most people miss, and go to their graves not knowing anything about.

So just as we do not realize the extent of our true identity in the invisible realm, and stick only to what we see in the mirror, neither do we realize that the church, Christianity, is only the outside -- the vessel carrying a cargo that is the truly precious material offered to us by the grace of God. The truth inherent in the revelation of Jesus is not found in ornaments, buildings or rituals, it is found in the spiritual awakening, the stirring within that it creates for us.

It seems that many people are satisfied with the external. It is comforting, habitual, familiar, nostalgic and sometimes it does indeed intensify that connection with the deeper realms. But make no mistake about it, we are not meant to stop at the surface, and quite often the surface keeps us from the deeper teachings. When religion is limited to that, we get superstition, simplistic thinking, half-truths, intolerance, and disconnection between science and religion, all of the fragmentation that we know so well.

So many highly educated people can't relate to religion because they only see that surface. Ironically, they don't see its true depths, and so reject what they think is religion or its teachings. This external religion also creates the separation between the wisdom teachings of different peoples. We come much closer together when the heart of the matter is unveiled, when the best of Hinduism and Islam and Christianity are uncovered, then we are dealing with people who love God.

We're not dealing with inculturated things, with prejudices of different times and places, we're dealing with the ecstatic love of God. Think of Rumi the poet, also known as Mevleven, whose delight in the reality of God caused him to dance spontaneously and it gave rise to the Dervishes of Sufism, the mystical dimension of Islam.

The same is true with Christianity. We see the televangelist quite often selling us something, trying to keep up their budget for the television programs, but we don't have presented to us the transforming, powerful truths that are at the heart of the Christian teaching.

It is astonishing to discover that, in the fourth century in the Egyptian desert, that kind of profoundly practical applicable teaching -- the teaching that can heal you of your psychic wounds -- was known and shared by great teachers like Isaac the Syrian or John Climacus who wrote "The Ladder of Divine Ascent." Down through the centuries these men and women were closely linked to the origins of the Faith. They shared a wisdom teaching that was extraordinarily potent and enabled people to truly connect with the spiritual dimension, with a spiritual reality that awakened them inwardly and made them more than they would have otherwise been. And that has been lost to us.

So we in the west grew up in an environment completely disconnected with the great teachings and insights of the early masters of the Faith, those spiritual guides, those spiritual directors and teachers that came down from the traditions of the Middle East, where Jesus walked, where his Apostles taught. We do find links down through history and those links between East and West are through the mystics in particular.

It is the lovers of God who believed in the experience of God -- in tasting and seeing -- that kept alive this flame of Truth that can be verified by your own experience. The last forty years, this is being rediscovered. Finally, there are translations of these ancient teachings available to us as we become one global community. All these lost or forgotten teachings are within our reach, so it is time for us to reclaim the wholeness of Christianity -- not the Middle Ages, not the Reformation, not the Puritans, but the whole spectrum of the Christian spiritual tradition that was meant to be ours. If you want inner freedom from your worries and fears, if you want to learn how to develop a compassion that takes you out of yourself, all of these are available. There is knowledge, a "gnosis" or inner knowledge about inner things that was at the heart of Christianity from the beginning.

In the second century, Clement of Alexandria, teaching of this gnosis, said that it would take three years for a new Christian to study before going to baptism. Now we baptize children without much thought. Yet there is a great science of the spirit to be shared, a psychotherapy if you will, that is alive and well and available to us. So you who seek for deep truth, for the mystery and sacredness of life, don't give up looking just because the externals seemed to be the opposite of what they should be. Keep searching, for it is to be found. You will find that pearl of great price, in fact you will be led to it.

So don't give up! One day, you will be given that which will set your heart on fire and you will become a new person, the person you were always meant to be.

7

Theosis
The Path of God-realization

Another one of the great teachings of Early Christianity is found in the central concept of Theosis. This term is at the heart of the theology and the mindset of the eastern Orthodox Church of the early centuries of Christianity.

Theosis is a dynamic term meaning deification, divinization, God-realization, glorification. We are called to enter an experience, that at the heart of this teaching, of this religion is *the experience of entering a new quality of consciousness.* One of the early teachers says: "God became man so that man might become God." This was orthodox Christianity. Let's understand this clearly; this is not one of those New Age ideas of "I Am God." No one was more in awe of the unknowability of the Uncreated One than the Orthodox teachings, but there was an understanding that we have a connection -- the image of God within. We are designed for that process, and that process can be understood in modern terms as a *change of consciousness.* We all know we have highs and lows, and sometimes we are more reasonable and have a better perspective.

Imagine if you could spend your life seeing everything as from a mountain -- the big picture, instead of being caught in the petty moment. It's like people who know they are dying, who are aware of their mortality, who suddenly have a whole new set of priorities. All of us can have that kind of wisdom, and all intuitions of humanity throughout history have called us to it, from the stoics to Carlos Castanedas -- the idea of remembering your death is found in all the philosophies and teachings throughout the world, because it awakens us to the significance of the moment, to what is really important, to the nobility of being, to the wonder of being alive.

It is possible for us to clear out the fog of worry, fear, anxiety and stress that we have taken for granted as how life should be, especially modern life with its hurried non-stop condition. People are in a constant state of stress, cut off from who they are really meant to be.

So, if we enter the reality of Christianity, we must realize, as it says in the second Letter of Peter, that we are called to become *partakers of (participants in) the divine nature.* That is not some inconceivable state of natural versus supernatural, but rather a realization that there is a whole spectrum of experience available to us, and that we shut ourselves down to the lowest possible measure when we cling to what seems to be the norm all around us, and fail to realize what there is to be found.

We all know people who are constantly negative, always complaining, and will go to their graves like that. Truly you know that this is no way to live. It's not why we were born. It's not why there are sunrises, sunsets and beauty around us. Through our awakened presence, our heightened consciousness, the universe becomes conscious of itself. Our seeing the beauty of the world makes that beauty more meaningful, more fully what it was called to be, and that is true in human lives all around, and in all that we do.

One philosopher says you can water a plant because it needs water, or you can water it with love. The Buddhist tea ceremony and other eastern insights help us enter the moment, enter the action, in a state of mind that is receptive and open to a vaster truth. All of us can get there, but we have our backs to it and we let ourselves be crushed by the affairs of life, by the external world. Another philosopher says we are stimulus response machines or mechanisms. We just react to life all the time, rather than proactively making conscious choices and acting upon them. We constantly respond like puppets on a string, and this is a truth that you can verify; something goes wrong, and all day long you react. Who you are in the morning and who you are at night don't match up because of all that has been going on.

You can't guarantee that you are the same person you'll be that evening, or whether you'll be filled with anger or distress. That's why this matter of inner peace is so important, because it lays a groundwork for that new life, that theosis, that transformation, that link with God, the ultimate destiny of our spirits -- not in the afterlife, but right here and now.

It's a matter of different degrees of consciousness. Seeing what it is that pulls us to the lower degrees of what is called *sleep*. Jesus speaks of, *"Wake, do not sleep!"* throughout the gospels. *"Awake O sleeper, arise from the dead and Christ will set you free,"* says Saint Paul.

These are not just metaphors. These are recognitions of our state, our condition. We are hypnotized by the outside world, pulled out of ourselves. We need to have an inner space that is separate, that is distinct from what is happening to us. In the ancient teachings it is called *hesychia*, inner tranquility, and it can be achieved, it is available to each of us if we know what efforts to make. We spoke of the watch of your heart, of self-awareness, of self-observation that begins to do triage in what is happening to us and eventually that creates an inner space, an inner separation.

It divides our attention so that we see the outside world and we're aware of ourselves -- so that we can maintain some quality of consciousness of attention within, that is undisturbed as it watches our thoughts and emotions, as it watches the outside world and begins to get stronger. This becomes the foundation for a new, more objective, more tranquil consciousness, capable of an act of will instead of the knee-jerk reaction that is standard, automatic behavior.

The early fathers and mothers teach us to seek that hesychia, that inner tranquility, where we are silent enough to hear from Spirit. Spirit is always trying to reach us. We're never listening to it, we're never receptive. Even in our prayers, we use so many words and express so many needs instead of just listening. Have you ever just sat in silence in mind and body, and listened?

The teachings tell us that we can listen in that way in the midst of chaos and noise. The famous Brother Lawrence of *The Practice of the Presence of God*, says that "Even in the midst of the pots and pans in the kitchen, I'm just like I am at the altar in communion on my knees in the chapel." He found that same inner place which can be silent, peaceful, controlled. That's where we find the birth of the fruits of the spirit: *love, joy, peace, patience, goodness, kindness, generosity, faithfulness and self-control.*

All of these can manifest and make us people who do good in this world, who are good incarnated into this world, and who bring so much fulfillment and joy, both to ourselves and to others, that life becomes meaningful and worthwhile. This is what is at the heart of the inner teachings of Christianity, beyond the surface of religion and rituals, in that place where each of us has to take responsibility and make those efforts so that we can cooperate with Grace, as Spirit itself leads us into new life.

That is the process of rebirth -- theosis. May you journey into that new consciousness and may you find the wisdom that can help you along the way. Know that it is available, it is not lost, and if you want it badly enough, you will find it.

8

Esotericism and Christianity

If you're one of those who wonders why Christianity has so often been its very opposite down through the centuries -- burning heretics, starting wars, creating violence in the world – then it's important that you understand that there are multiple dimensions to a spiritual teaching. They've been known down through time as the *exoteric* -- the outer, the outside, the superficial; the *mesoteric* -- the middle, the normal arrangement of its good, but limited understanding, and the *esoteric*.

Now the expression *esoteric* has often been portrayed as secretive and even occult, but that's not what it means. Esoteric means "inner." All of us begin with that outer range and need to individually find our way and discover the inner depths of the teaching, to make it our own. Over the centuries, people have often been stuck only at the surface level, and never even searched into the real meaning for their own transformation.

So they saw religion as a cultural phenomenon, followed the rituals, and were satisfied with that limited version of religion. Today, we often separate spirituality and religion because of that very incrusted, outdated and institutionalized aspect of what should be a dynamic, living teaching. So in every generation each of us must rediscover for ourselves what the esoteric is, what the real inner meaning is that organically shapes a human being and causes the experiences that have been enshrined as doctrine. By that I mean that the mystics, the lovers of God, have attempted to explain their experience. The idea of the trinity, developed by be Gregory of Nyssa was a failed attempt in some ways, certainly down through the centuries, to express a mystical experience of the communion, the union of energies from the Uncreated One through the incarnation -- this community of love that so few people have managed to understand. It was poetry, not theology.

As with everything else, human beings take something and reduce it to its lowest common denominator, and often create the very opposite of what it is meant to mean. So each of us is responsible, is accountable for searching out what it is that is at the heart of a wisdom teaching, a spiritual teaching.

We have separated esoteric from the mainstream, and yet the early teachers who taught the monastics in the deserts of Egypt and Syria, the descendants of the apostles, were merely trying to be authentic in developing the purity of heart that Jesus spoke of – *"Blessed are the pure in heart, for these will see God."* Jesus himself makes it clear, and the words are recorded: *"That the secret of the kingdom has been given to you, but not to them, that I speak in parables to them."* There is an outer and there is an inner that must be discovered by effort, not just handed over. Otherwise, it is received by a limited part of ourselves as opposed to being hungered after and absorbed in a way that creates *Metanoia* - change of mind, metamorphosis.

So Christianity has been reduced to this cultural thing, this milk toast version of itself, and in many ways has betrayed the Savior and crucified him again by its misrepresentation and misunderstandings of the teachings. Oftentimes it has been guilty of the very thing Jesus said to the Pharisees – *"You stand at the gates of the kingdom and do not enter, and do not allow others to enter either."* In this day and age, when religions from around the world are made known and surfacing, it is critical that we rediscover the origins, the source, the roots of what shaped western civilization, so that we can separate that which is exoteric from that which is esoteric, and find the living teaching that changes lives. Each of us must walk this narrow path, which is fraught with crevices, wrong directions, deceptions, manipulations and obstacles, both from ourselves and from the world around us.

You know that those who are detractors of Christianity often reduce it to a version of Christianity that is inaccurate, which is seen on television perhaps, but not understood. In other words, the detractors don't take the time to find out what it is that they are condemning. They see the surface thing and have no idea of the deep waters from which it comes.

So I urge you not to make that mistake, for this could be what you have been looking for all along, *if* you enter into what it really is. We must explore that inner dimension of Christianity, the esotericism, the mysticism that is from the beginning, where Jesus says: "I and the Father are One." He is speaking mystically. To reduce it to some rational concept, with some social gospel idea, is to do what Judas did to Jesus. Judas wanted to take care of the existential needs of the poor right now, and take the spiritual revelation, the universal expression of God's truth, and make it a social agenda. Since the nineteenth century, many folks have gone with that extremely limited understanding of the gospel and in many ways made nonsense out of it. For instance, when Jesus says, "Blessed are the poor," he is saying: "Blessed are the poor *in spirit.*" He is referring to those who have humbled themselves. He is not speaking to an economic class. What a violation of a profound teaching! So each of us must get past these errors, these confusions, these muddied waters, to find the true pearl that will make of us the best that we are meant to be, to make of us an incarnation of goodness and a spiritual presence and strength and clarity, and give us the capacity to help the Creator care for the creation.

Down through history, the one unitive line of understanding has been through the mystics, the true lovers of God, so often misunderstood, and perhaps always misunderstood. The great Meister Eckhart was excommunicated. Recently, the Pope turned that around, because it was so grievous an error. Again, as Eckhart's student, John Tyler, said to his detractors at that time: "You understood him from the point of your time, but he was speaking to you from the point of view of eternity."

138

There are different levels of wisdom, of understanding, of consciousness, and each of us must search in order to find them. Jesus says it clearly -- Seek, ask -- and therefore it is a true journey. It may take a lifetime, but it will change everything. So before you reject things, before you mock things, take another look, let spirit resonate in your soul.

Pray for help and guidance, open yourself, be receptive. You know that a negative mind, a cynical mind, will not find any truth. Negativity, by its very nature, is a lie, say the wise ones, and in truth, you know that is the case. We hear one part of what we want to hear to make the worst of it. It justifies wrong behavior, it poisons us physically and psychically, and it causes destruction in the world and in other lives.

Negativity runs the world, say the philosophers. Not money or sex, but negativity, because we feel sometimes perversely more alive in those dark energies. But Spirit will not enter that coarseness. We must be in a higher state to communicate, to encounter Spirit, to even know there is such a dimension.

And so Jesus leads us into it through timeless images and stories, all of which are containers of deep, unfathomable cosmic Truth -- Truth that through a lifetime will still need to be explored and will bring new riches of understanding. So don't be afraid of that word esotericism, rather, let it invite you into the spiritually mature call, to where the meat is, not the milk for infants.

"Once I thought like a child," as Paul says. Now it is high time to authentically find what these teachings are. They are not a building, they are not a middle class or a social agenda or your grandmother's version of it, or some twisted mix of patriotism. It is wisdom from the Holy, which from the beginning has been abused and its followers persecuted, because those who cannot understand it, turn against it.

Jesus says, *"If they persecuted me, they will persecute you,"* and this goes right into the churches, where persecutions of the worst kinds often take place. So it's a lonely road, but you'll find companions along the way, and those precious friends, those spiritual friends, who make life worthwhile. So be not afraid, seek and you will find.

9

Holiness

What does it means to seek to be holy? In the scriptures, we find that the description of people who gather together -- the Assembly of the Faithful, the Church, those who are seeking God -- are "Holy and Beloved," says Paul in the letter to the Colossians at chapter three.

Now these words are universal words, meant for you and me today, not merely for the first century. And in this secular, materialistic world of ours, so distant from the societies that sensed the sacred, the mystery, and the wonder of life, that word "holy" has been so abused that it's very hard to understand it in a practical way.

Most of us have no interest in being holy. So, let's understand what the teaching is. The "holy" in Greek *hagios, kodesh* in Hebrew -- comes from an ancient Assyrian word which means purified or purification. So holiness has something to do with purification, and again most of us have no interest in that sort of thing. We've left behind those ways; they're unfamiliar, they don't make sense, and they don't fit into the twenty-first century.

But I would suggest to you, in a very down to earth way, that purification means *freeing ourselves of violence.* "Cleansing the inside of the cup," as Jesus says -- cleansing our psychology of all that negativity and its myriad of forms that bring us down into a miserable existence. Now, purification, holiness, is getting close to home. If you're constantly living in fear and worry and anger, it's like having toxic chemicals inside of you, literally.

Most of us know that our blood pressure goes up when we get angry; that the adrenalin is burning through us, creating other chemicals that are poisonous to our inner organs. People die of heart attacks from wrong thinking and feeling, and from reacting to situations in negative ways that they don't have to choose. Purification is the best kind of therapy you could hope for concerning your health. In this world full of infomercials about diets and how to get your body in shape, where billions of dollars are spent on that industry, the true approach to health and wholeness is spiritual. If you are free from being embarrassed all the time, free from worry about what people think, and if you are truly free and happy to be alive, all that other business takes its proper place in your life. Because if you lose all the weight that is such a burden to you, that society frowns on, and still have stomach cramps from this kind of wrong thinking, from constantly getting angry and, like some folks I know, ending up in the emergency room on a regular basis, you haven't done anything to get healthy. So if we must put holiness as a concept in our twenty-first century little box, health, well being, and caring for oneself is very much at the center of it. But, of course it is much bigger than that. It's not about us. It's about enabling our blossoming so we can be useful to the universe.

Let's take that word a little further. Holiness comes from the English "Hal" meaning wholeness, and if you tie that word to the word "salvation" – "sozo" in Greek which means "healing" -- suddenly it's something that can make sense to us, and not just some mysterious pious term that doesn't fit our reality. In fact, holiness is at the center of reality. It is we who have entered the world of fantasy and illusion, and wander about like blind people, banging into things, constantly running into dead ends, and allowing ourselves to fall into pits of despair, anger and depression, and all those things that ruin our life.

Jesus came into the world; wisdom comes into the world; God is in the world to give us a way out of that wrong living, unhappy living, that violent living. Do you know what will clean up society? What will enable people to get along? What will overcome domestic violence? What will allow us to care for our children? It all begins with spiritual cleanliness. Each of us has to take responsibility for ourselves, for how we live, for who we are. Until that happens, no system, no law, is going to solve the problem. If you want to help the earth, begin right here.

An example of this comes from our experience on airplanes, when we're told that when that oxygen mask comes down, we have to first put it on ourselves before we help our child. We must *have* oxygen before we can *give* oxygen. So we have to fix ourselves. We have to look within and see how dirty we are. What's the point of a good shower, washing your hair, then walking out into the world with a heart full of hate? What is going to cleanse that? That's what religion is about, and that's what these teachings are about. So don't allow the prejudices of the secular world, of atheism, to mock religion and try to reduce it to doctrines, myths, hypocrisy and silly rituals.

"Religion," which means *linking to God*, has to do with the heart of your life. Nothing less. It has been hijacked down through history, and now more than ever, by all kinds of deviant ways of thinking, by hucksters and salesmen and simple-minded folks who misrepresent it. But if you're truly seeking, Spirit will lead you to where you can find that which is real. In every generation, each of us has to rediscover the Truth that Christ brings into the world. We can't just assume that we know what it is or that others know what it is. We have to go on that journey ourselves, we have to stumble along and find the path that takes us beyond the human errors that have so damaged religion and the hope for humanity.

We look at history and we see what a bloody mess religion has made of it; we all know that can't be right, that that's not what Jesus came into the world for. And instead of just walking away from it all, we have to take responsibility ourselves. If you're the only one who understands that it's about becoming capable of love, of unconditional love, of transcending ourselves, our animal natures and our petty natures; if nobody else can figure that out except you, then you *be that one,* because the world needs you and God needs you in this dark time and place. It has always been dark, and most often those who have found the Truth have been martyred. Yet those who have found the Truth have also been filled with bliss, fulfilled and awakened to the true purpose of life.

This is available to you. You can become the whole person, the healthy person, the awakened person, the enlightened person that you were designed to be. The instructions are there. Don't let other people interpret them for you, find them for yourself. And then, day after day, you will begin to live a new life -- moment by moment. It is worth it more than anything else, because all of our problems come back to how we choose to behave, how we are capable of functioning, how we relate to others. If we resolve that, and bring to it what the New Testament teaches -- clothe yourself with compassion, put on the mind of Christ, put your mind on things that are above -- if that becomes real to us, everything changes for us. When the inner changes, the outer follows suit. Don't wait for the outer to change first. Work on that inner life and you will see miracle in your life. You will be brought into the light, which is the purpose of religion and spirituality -- relationship, connectedness with Spirit and with all living things. May you find your way.

10

Seeking Peace in a Violent World

Everyone knows that many of the worst horrors of human history have taken place in the name of religion. To this day, people kill, maim, and hate in the name of their version of God. Yet, most spiritual teachings originated around the concept of peace and peacemaking. Christ's call to "love your enemies" is a revolutionary challenge for human evolution. Islam's "surrender" and "remembrance of God the Compassionate," should lead to a similar quality of being.

These wisdom teachings, from revealers of the Divine Will, are so powerful that humanity surrounded them with all the trappings of what we name "religion." In the process, their original purpose was lost sight of, which was to lead human beings out of their sub-animal tendencies for brutal violence, and toward a capacity for goodness and compassion.

No one can deny that little has changed from the barbarism of the ancient world to the headlines of today's news. Men, in particular, continue to be as ferocious and savage as they were in the days of Attila the Hun. Our modern advancements have done nothing to transform the human potential for bestial behavior, and after two thousand years, religion has yet to fulfill its purpose of guiding people toward inner and outer peace.

Consider the words of Father Alphonse Goettmann, a French Orthodox priest and author of several books on the transforming purpose of Christianity:

"With regard to Christianity, its history is indeed filled with conflicts: judgments, exclusions, inquisitions, prisons, wars and crusades ... There is only one problem: it is to believe that Christianity is a religion, a system in the midst of others, which inevitably results in inclusion or exclusion, which distorts all relationships and has strictly nothing to make with the Gospel! It is religion and its representatives who killed Christ ... Christ came to abolish religion, this is His 'Great Work.' Religion is necessary when there is a wall which separates God from human beings. We are here, God is elsewhere, so it is necessary then to have a religion to connect us to God. But the Christ, who is at the same time human and divine, reversed the wall which separated us. He brought a new life, not a new religion ... That is really the center of the Christian Faith."

It is this faith, this knowing, that gives birth to inner freedom, confident joy, indomitable hope, and radiant love for all other beings. This is what the man from Nazareth came to tell us, and it is the very simplicity of his cosmic message that got him nailed to a cross. In the light of that pure, unadulterated, and overwhelming experience of the goodness of God, all the complexity, arrogance, and thirst for power found in human history down through the ages, is revealed for the tragic and shameful emptiness that it is.

In this age of global interrelatedness and hunger for meaning, it is incumbent upon persons driven by a need to find and manifest peace, to find that which is universal and practical at the core of all spiritual teachings. A Tibetan Buddhist can be enriched by the wisdom of the Christ just as a Christian can develop a deeper inner practice through a study of Islamic mysticism.

Our epoch can no longer accept the artificial walls that have stood for centuries between peoples and cultures. This is a new century, and there is no going back. The validity of religion is now measured by its value to human development, not by a rigid belief system that is so often used as a battering ram against other groups. The criteria for identifying the worth of religious teachings beneath the crust of history and institutions are found in their potential for transforming a self-centered nature into one that is radiant with unbounded compassion.

Each of us is meant to come face to face with the depths of our being and awaken to our greatest fulfillment: becoming conscious children of the universe, incarnating the unconditional love that created us all. All religion is a roadmap. History, human error, and institutional structures have turned the map into the treasure, thereby forgetting its true intent.

The violence in our world will never be changed until individuals have changed, and individuals will never change until religion as inner transformation has penetrated to the hearts of their beings and made them into new persons. Change happens one human being at a time. It is your transformation, my transformation, that will make a difference in this wondrous but troubled world of ours, as we become who we truly are beyond the mundane limitations of the narrow realities in which we function.

19581784R00092

Printed in Great Britain
by Amazon